MANAGING
TO STAY OUT OF
COURT

MANAGING
TO STAY OUT OF
COUR

HOW TO AVOID THE
8 DEADLY SINS
OF MISMANAGEMENT

JATHAN JANOVE, ESQ.

Society for Human Resource Management
Alexandria, Virginia
USA

Berrett-Koehler Publishers, Inc.
San Francisco
USA

This book is published by the Society for Human Resource Management (SHRM®) and Berrett-Koehler Publishers, Inc. The interpretations, conclusions, and recommendations in this book are those of the author and do not necessarily represent those of the publishers.

ORDERING INFORMATION
Quantity sales. Special discounts are available on quantity purchases. For details, contact SHRM at SHRMStore@SHRM.org or the "Special Sales Department" at the Berrett-Koehler, address above.
Orders for college textbook/course adoption use. Please contact Berrett-Koehler.
Orders by U.S. trade bookstores and wholesalers. Please contact Publishers Group West, 1700 Fourth Street, Berkeley, CA 94710. Tel: (510) 528-1444; Fax (510) 528-3444.

The Society for Human Resource Management (SHRM) is the world's largest association devoted to human resource management. Representing more than 175,000 individual members, the Society serves the needs of HR professionals by providing the most essential and comprehensive set of resources available. As an influential voice, SHRM is committed to advancing the human resource profession to ensure that HR is an essential and effective partner in developing and executing organizational strategy. Visit SHRM Online at www.shrm.org.

Library of Congress Cataloging-in-Publication Data

Janove, Jathan W., 1958-
Managing to stay out of court : how to avoid the 8 deadly sins of mismanagement / Jathan W. Janove.
        p. cm.
Includes bibliographical references and index.
ISBN 1-57675-318-2
1. Industrial relations. 2. Management. 3. Leadership. I. Title.

HD6971.J36 2005
658—dc22

                              2004020051

Printed in the United States of America.
10 9 8 7 6 5 4 3 2 1

Contents

Contents, continued

Preface

CONFESSIONS OF AN EMPLOYMENT LAWYER...

My start in the employment law field occurred in the summer of 1980. I worked as a law student in a legal aid clinic on the south side of Chicago. My first case involved representing a discharged hospital worker who insisted that he was a victim of discrimination based either on race or his "good looks." At this time, and for some years thereafter, I primarily represented employees pursuing claims of race, sex, and other forms of employment discrimination and, as the new concept took flight, sexual harassment. As the 1980s unfolded, my practice became mixed, representing employees in some cases, employers in others, a union here, management there. Since the early 1990s, however, I have represented management exclusively.

Over the years, I observed that in the vast majority of claims, the employee eventually gave up, the employer prevailed, or the two parties settled the claim for a small amount of money. So what's all the fuss about workplace litigation, I wondered? If the odds are overwhelming that employers will not get burned in a lawsuit no matter how poorly they manage, why worry? Upon reflection, some reasons surfaced:

1. Employers do occasionally get hit hard in the legal system. Some have been forced into bankruptcy over major employment litigation. The fear is palpable.

2. Even a successful claim defense can cost six figures. And this doesn't include the countless hours, energy, and anxiety expended by company employees involved in the litigation process. After the successful conclusion of a lawsuit, a client once said, "I'm not suggesting you aren't expensive. However, you aren't nearly as expensive as I am."

3. By the time a claim has been filed, the employer has usually already paid a terrific price in workplace morale and productivity. Plus, once a claim has been filed, the odds of mending the workplace relationship are virtually nil.

Following the explosion of employment litigation in the 1990s, I became intrigued with the question of claim prevention. Can an employer swim against the tide of an increasingly litigious, victim-oriented society? Can tough management decisions be made and executed without producing claims? Despite the decade's 1991 Civil Rights Act, Americans with Disabilities Act, Family Medical Leave Act, and expansion of exceptions to the at-will rule, can an employer nevertheless manage a workforce without interference from the legal system?

In working with clients, I learned that claim prevention did not require rocket science, or even great managerial talent. Rather, claim prevention required consistent application of a few basic principles. I then began to ponder whether the bar could be set higher, whether one could simultaneously achieve claim prevention and people leadership.

As a teenager in the early 1970s, I sometimes tagged along when my father conducted workshops on community and organizational development. He occasionally allowed me to participate in workshops focusing on improved communication, trust, and teamwork. Not surprising, these experiences receded in memory after I became a litigator. Now, however, I started exploring whether employers could take the same steps to avoid claims and improve morale, productivity, and retention. I began studying management and organizational development experts who do not deal with employment law or workplace claims. People like Peter Drucker, W. Edwards Deming, Spencer Johnson, Ken Blanchard, Tom Peters, Stephen Covey, and Peter Collins are not lawyers and say little or nothing about workplace claim prevention. Nevertheless, I explored how their ideas might prove useful for claim-prevention purposes. I also began to take a closer look at my own "lousy" clients—employers that generate meager legal fees for me yet are themselves highly profitable. Finally, I had opportunities to act as a manager myself and experience firsthand the painful distinction between practice and preaching.

Managing to Stay Out of Court and the Eight Deadly Sins and their corresponding Virtues grow directly out of this research, reflection, and experience. First developed as a training program in 1997, the Sins and Virtues constitute my attempt to show managers how to achieve one-stop shopping—that is, to lead, mentor, and develop employees while keeping the lawyers at bay.

Sincere thanks go to those who contributed to the development of this book: Wendy Bliss, J.D., SPHR, for her astute and helpful review of the manuscript, and my publisher, Laura Lawson, whom I would recommend to any first-time author. Throughout the process, she has provided ideas, insight, encouragement, and a deft use of carrot and stick. I also want to thank the following individuals who come from the fields of HR, employment law, and corporate management, and formed a collective brain trust for me: Cherie Aldana, Lois Baar, Scott Baxter, Bruce Bracken, Bill Campbell, Mark Holland, Jim Isaacson, Max Neves, and Mike O'Brien, the last of whom prodded me to write this book and insisted that its value would eclipse the effort—no matter how many billable hours it cost me!

Finally, I want to thank my wife, Marjorie, and my children, Gabrielle, Raphael, and Nathaniel, for their support, encouragement, and tolerance—and for reminding me that the lessons of this book don't just apply in the workplace.

Introduction

"Common sense is not so common."

—Voltaire

DOES THE STORY THAT FOLLOWS SOUND FAMILIAR? What goes wrong, even when management has the best of intentions? Why do employees sue their employers, long after wreaking havoc in workplace morale and productivity? What can be done?

The Promotion Turns Sour

The first-time manager's new promotion excited her. She had goals. She made plans. Unlike the managers whose failings she had experienced first-hand, she knew how to treat employees. She would make the word "team" a reality in her department.

Six months later, however, her enthusiasm had faded. Frustration had set in. Employees had not responded to her direction as she had envisioned. She had had an angry confrontation with a subordinate and did not get support from senior management and HR for the discipline she wished to impose. Two employees she hired had not lived up to expectations. One of her best employee's attendance, attitude, and performance had inexplicably declined. She noticed that she had begun to lapse into the behavior of past managers of whom she had been so critical. She avoided problem employees, told white lies, and let problems build to the eruption point. Worst of all, one of her employees accused her of gender and race discrimination in a claim he filed with the Equal Employment Opportunity Commission. Yet despite her lifelong commitment to fair employment principles, company lawyers opined that the claim had "substantial settlement value." "Management wouldn't be such a bad job," she thought ruefully, "if only there weren't employees to manage!"

The Basic Instinct: Avoidance

This book answers the questions at the start of this chapter in a unique way. It zeros in on a universal culprit: *the instinct to avoid.* Being responsible for the efforts of a disparate group of personalities, temperaments, strengths, and weaknesses is a challenge for any manager. The instinct to avoid is a natural, self-protective outgrowth of the anxiety the challenge produces. It results in under-communicating, putting space between manager and employee, and maintaining distance in workplace relationships. Fear of unpleasant encounters, of being the bearer of bad tidings, of being vulnerable, or of being unable to predict outcomes leads to a lack of both praise and criticism, to less speaking and even less listening. Problems build, mistrust increases, and opportunities for improvement slip by.

The times when the instinct to avoid is strongest are usually the times when doing the opposite would be most beneficial to both employee and manager. When managers are worried about an employee heading in the wrong direction or when their department faces major challenges are the very times when they most need to communicate openly, honestly, and candidly. Yet the managers' instinct induces them to do the opposite.

The Instinct to Avoid and Brainlock

The world of employment litigation provides a window through which we can learn how workplace relationships break down. Pleadings, discovery, and depositions tell stories of how otherwise resolvable workplace problems degenerate into anger, bitterness, and a desire to take revenge through the U.S. legal system. Regardless of the nature of the claim, employee anger is the catalyst. It takes the form of "brainlock," a condition that occurs when employees become so upset with their employer that their thoughts get "locked up" and they cannot move forward emotionally or psychologically without striking back at the cause of their pain. Brainlock produces a variety of workplace evils, including violence, sabotage, disloyalty, theft, and defamation. However, it most frequently takes the form of a claim or lawsuit filed against the employer.

What produces brainlock? Mean-spirited, ogre-like managers? Or decent, well-meaning men and women who struggle to manage challenging employees? The answer in almost every case is the latter. Ironically, conscientious managers who sincerely desire the success and welfare of their employees most often create brainlock. What leads them astray? It's the natural, self-protective instinct to avoid.

What This Book Sets Out to Do

If one distilled the essence of the Eight Deadly Sins of Mismanagement and corresponding Eight Virtues, it would be the conversion of the instinct to avoid into *a trigger for doing the opposite*—even when the threat of a lawsuit exists. Beginning with Chapter One's opening story of the manager who learns how to ski and thus learns how to manage, the Sins and Virtues pair up to harness this instinct for good ends and, as a whole, to create a foundation for effective people leadership. Unlike most management books, this one addresses strategies for moving directly from theory to practice, for lifting the lessons off the page and transporting them into the workplace. The goal here is not to write a book that makes a satisfying read. It's to produce *results*.

The Sins and Virtues Summarized

Chapter One:
The First Sin, Managing Like a Beginning Skier
The First Virtue, Weight Forward on Skis
Using the analogy of learning how to ski, this chapter shows how managers can convert the instinct to avoid into a trigger to do the opposite.

Subjects addressed include preventing workplace violence, dealing with sexual harassment, using the initial employment period, and how to become a star employee.

Chapter Two:
The Second Sin, Dissin' Your Employees
The Second Virtue, D-I-S'ng Your Employees
At first glance, the Sin and corresponding Virtue look the same. However, the two could not be more different. The former has to do with unintentionally insulting employees and causing brainlock. The second is a method of communication that effectively insulates managers from committing this Sin. By being Direct, Immediate, and Specific with employees, managers create a climate of mutual respect even during the most difficult times in a workplace relationship.

Subjects addressed include "gunnysack" management, use of e-mail, workplace violence, praising employees, self-help and anti-harassment training, D-I-S'ng in writing, managing a diverse workforce, and putting a battery in the D-I-S method.

Chapter Three:
The Third Sin, Rationalizing Away Truth
The Third Virtue, Making Honesty the Only Policy
Why do managers who prize honesty and integrity lie to employees? This chapter explores why well-meaning managers commit this Sin, the common rationalizations in which they engage, why such dishonesty is harmful even when motives are pure, and what to substitute for rationalization.

Subjects addressed include discharge, performance evaluations, family businesses, surreptitious recordings of conversations, when to get legal advice, and the dismiss-and-redirect technique.

Chapter Four:
The Fourth Sin, Misguided Benevolence;
The Fourth Virtue, E-R-A—Expectations,
Responsibility, and Accountability

Empathy is an important strength in a manager. Yet when compassion for an employee with significant health or personal needs induces the manager to abandon expectations and accountability, the manager helps no one, *including the employee*. Rather, the manager's E-R-A must be maintained at all times, for everyone's sake.

Subjects addressed include a surprise ADA claim, severance agreements, reasonable accommodation and performance standards, worker's compensation, and the game of "management baseball."

Chapter Five:
The Fifth Sin, Falling into the Inconsistency Trap
The Fifth Virtue, Ducks in a Row

Four types of inconsistency cause brainlock and lead to legal trouble: (1) person to person, or treating an employee inconsistently with another employee; (2) person to document, or treating an employee inconsistently with a written document such as a performance evaluation or employee handbook provision; (3) document to document, or having workplace or personnel documents inconsistent with each other; and (4) person over time, or treating an employee inconsistently with how the person has been treated in the past.

Subjects addressed include conducting an employment litigation post-mortem; subjective and objective inconsistency; key questions to get ducks in a row; preventing discrimination and retaliation claims; dealing with workplace change; the "that was then, this is now" message; and offering employees amnesty.

Chapter Six:
The Sixth Sin, Letting Employees Speculate
The Sixth Virtue, Open Information Channels

The Sixth Sin triggers the Law of Employee Speculation, meaning that what employees don't know, they will speculate about, and their speculation will invariably assume the worst. Chapter Six provides several examples of the Law of Employee Speculation in action. It also describes the benefits employers enjoy when they shift their paradigm from guardian of information to disseminator of information.

Subjects addressed include conducting terminations, avoiding wrongful discharge claims, layoff planning, and changing to an information-rich company culture.

Chapter Seven:
The Seventh Sin, Listening Through Your "I"
The Seventh Virtue, Listening Through Your Ears

Managers who listen through their "I"s keep their egos foremost as they adopt one of three methods of listening to their employees: (1) the Toe-Tappers—for whom listening means waiting to talk; (2) the Autobiographers—who translate everything they hear into their own experiences or beliefs; and (3) the Cross-Examiners—who listen until they find the employee weakness on which to pounce. By contrast, managers who learn to listen through their ears instead of their egos experience great benefits, including gaining understanding that would otherwise have seemed impossible, correcting dangerously false assumptions, and learning of opportunities that can be beneficially exploited.

Subjects addressed include mediation; internal investigations; administering discipline based on a learning principle; the two-for-one or God's hint, E-A-R, funnel, directive listening, Monk, and Triple Two techniques; and applying the Seventh Virtue in the home.

Chapter Eight:
The Eighth Sin, Front-of-the-Nose Perspective
The Eighth Virtue, the Big Picture

This Sin/Virtue pair involves a basic way of thinking about one's role as a manager. When managers develop a Big Picture focus—taking into account who we are, what we are, and where we are going—and use it as the framework for all significant communications with employees, they move from managers to leaders. A Big Picture perspective inexorably leads managers away from the Sins and toward the Virtues.

Subjects addressed include managing a diverse workforce; extricating oneself from potential discrimination claims; dealing with the EEOC; creating a Big Picture outline and Star Profile; HR as strategic partner and management coach; questions to identify mission, vision, values, and goals; and the Campfire Technique.

Chapter Nine:
Moving from Sin to Virtue

A book about management Sins and Virtues may make for good reading. However, it won't accomplish much if managerial behavior and habits do not change. This chapter addresses specific strategies for achieving transfer of training. To produce meaningful, sustained change, the reader must make a commitment to an ongoing process, including improving existing habits and replacing Sins with Virtues. For those willing to make such a change, this chapter provides strategies, steps, and techniques designed to transfer theory into practice.

Subjects addressed include individual change strategies, companywide change strategies, soliciting employee feedback, planning and executing a training program, and aligning systems with change.

Appendix: Tools to Help You Move from Sin to Virtue

To assist the motivated reader with the change process, the Appendix contains several forms and checklists, including samples culled from actual workplace situations.

CHAPTER 1

The First Sin:
Managing Like a Beginning Skier

"A fellow is more afraid of the trouble he might have than he ever is of the trouble he's already got. He'll cling to the trouble he's used to before he'll risk a change."

—William Faulkner, Light in August

THE FIRST SIN OF MISMANAGEMENT ARISES from managers' desire to avoid potential trouble by accepting the trouble they've already got—with the result that they only make matters worse. In this respect, they are comparable to beginning skiers who likewise possess a desire or instinct to avoid trouble—in this case, the downhill slope. Yet by allowing this natural self-protective instinct to control their actions, beginning skiers lean back, doing the *opposite* of what is necessary to ski safely and effectively. The anxious skier thus parallels the anxious manager.

Leaning Back on Problems

Numerous experiences with employment litigation reveal an irony: leaning back to avoid trouble or lawsuits actually *increases* risk. There is perhaps no greater way to increase the risk of an unintended education in the legal system than by continually leaning back on your skis and avoiding or ignoring problems because your instinct tells you there will be trouble if you deal with them.

The protection that such avoidance offers is illusory. Employment litigation arises in many ways other than a supervisor's direct action against an employee. The explosion of harassment litigation is one example. In these cases, management inaction plays a critical role. The failure to respond to early reports of unwelcome workplace conduct leads to the creation of a "hostile environment" and to employer liability for failure to take reasonable preventive or remedial action.

In failing to discipline employees who strike them as potential plaintiffs, managers effectively encourage these staff members to repeat and intensify the negative behaviors that signaled the problem. Eventually, the dam bursts and management takes action. By then, the employee's anger has increased to the point of brainlock, and he or she files a claim or lawsuit. Once an employee files a claim, management's long avoidance of the problem makes defending against the claim more difficult, since there is a major question about why long-tolerated negative behavior suddenly became unacceptable. Thus, rather than creating a safe harbor, the instinct to avoid litigation helps pave the way to the legal system. As you read the following stories of workplace problems and disputes, some of which ended up in court, observe the connection between the beginning-skier instinct and the employers' unwitting steps that put the companies there.

The Beginning Skier

Sally Jones manages an accounting department in Pittsburgh. While on vacation in Colorado, she decides to learn how to ski. To Sally, the bunny hill is the face of Everest. As happens with every new skier, a natural protective instinct kicks in.

Sally fears the downhill slope and the possibility of skiing too fast, losing control, and crashing. Her instinct tells her to counterbalance downhill momentum with uphill momentum. So she stands up straight on her skis and leans back, bringing her body closer to the uphill slope. Soon, however, Sally discovers that her instinct has betrayed her. As she struggles to her feet and brushes off the snow, she ponders, what now?

Unwittingly, Sally just skied the way she manages two employees back at the office. One is Kevin, a talented accountant who nonetheless has a short fuse and has been grousing about defects in the new computer system. Several employees complained to Sally in the past about Kevin's abusive or demeaning behavior. They now complain that he purposely resists performing certain tasks because he feels the new computer system will render his efforts meaningless. Another of Sally's employees is Mary, whose attendance and performance have had a few modest peaks but many deep valleys. Sally sees Mary's disappointing behavior, but she can't forget the fact that Mary previously filed a grievance against Sally's predecessor, asserting a "hostile environment."

Several times Sally has thought about having serious, sit-down discussions with her problem employees. But then Kevin's aggressive style and Mary's prior grievance come to mind, and she puts the meetings off until a "better time." She finds it much easier to address problems with her nonthreatening employees than to correct her problem employees.

When it comes to Kevin and Mary, Sally's self-protective instincts kick in. Her two employees assume the dimensions of Everest, so Sally leans back on her skis. She counterbalances her fear of plunging into an ugly confrontation with Kevin or being sued by Mary by putting protective space between herself and these workplace dangers. Just as on the ski slope, however, her leaning away from the challenge prevents her from resolving it successfully and greatly increases the risk of a painful crash.

Avoidable Violence Not Avoided

A company manufactured a highly sophisticated commercial food-processing system with fully loaded systems selling for upwards of a quarter-million dollars. Parts alone accounted for tens of thousands of dollars per sale. The company organized sales into two departments: Systems and Parts. A new CFO decided the company could boost sales by increasing competition between the two departments. He devised an incentive compensation plan that essentially created a zero-sum game between the two groups. The more commissions Systems earned, the fewer Parts earned, and vice versa.

The CFO got his wish for increased competition—but in ways he did not anticipate. First, the two departments stopped sharing information with each other. Next, reports surfaced that employees in one department were spying on the other, including slipping into offices and reviewing hardcopy and computer files. Finally, rumors flew that employees in Parts had conspired against Systems by helping a competitor sell a system to a prospective customer with several of Parts' parts, cutting Systems entirely out of the deal. The Systems department manager confronted his counterpart in Parts. The two men unleashed months' worth of frustration, mistrust, and anger. One of the managers then went after the other with a hammer. The company called in law enforcement and medical personnel; employment attorneys eventually followed.

Analysis showed that several months had elapsed between the first signs of trouble and the managers' violent confrontation. Employees and management were aware of the growing mistrust and tension. Warning sign after warning sign surfaced—blocked information, internal spying, departments actively undermining each other. Yet no one acted to head off the crisis. The instinct to lean back on skis paralyzed the company's leadership. The more negative, stressful, and dangerous the situation became, the more management's reluctance to deal with it increased. The instinct to lean back on skis became so strong that even after the disastrous confrontation between Systems and Parts, the company's executives chose not to confront the problems inherent in the incentive compensation plan since "we have already suffered enough trauma." They clung to the trouble they had rather than risk a change.

Leaning Back on Opportunity

Opportunities have something in common with problems: they involve uncertainty. There is no guarantee that investing in any employee, much less a problematic one, will produce a positive return. Yet most managers don't even try. The uncertainty of success triggers their managerial instinct to lean back on skis in order to protect themselves. As a result, just as problems are not solved, opportunities are not exploited. The protective instinct thwarts progress.

A Young Lawyer Finds the Right Fit

Just out of law school, a young attorney joined a prestigious law firm as a junior associate. Full of ambition and high expectations, he plunged into his new job. All did not go well, however. Bright and talented, but unseasoned and with a tendency toward abrasiveness when stressed, the attorney made mistakes and soon realized that a number of partners avoided giving him projects and did not train, coach, or mentor him. Over time, his embitterment and eroding self-confidence intensified the cycle of mistakes and abrasiveness, and the partners avoided him even more. Eventually, he left. The firm collectively shrugged him off as a waste of talent—while he shrugged off his first employer as rotten luck.

The lawyer found a job with another prestigious firm, arriving with the same strengths and weaknesses. The difference, however, was the way the two law firms viewed this mix. The former focused on the negatives and drew away from him, whereas the latter saw more potential than imperfection. It actively mentored the young attorney, helping him develop his talent while making it clear the abrasiveness had to go. This time, the lawyer thrived—in the same field, in the same type of job, and doing the same type of work as at his first employer. He eventually became a partner, highly regarded in the legal community and a source of prestige and excellent clients for his law firm.

Why such a huge difference when the lawyer's qualities, the job, and everything else were the same? The first law firm missed a crucial point: employee problems are often opportunities in disguise. The "waste of talent" could have developed into as valuable a contributor at the first firm as at the second. However, this was not possible because at the first sign of difficulty, the first firm began avoiding the problem. The instinct to avoid, to keep its weight back on skis, not only prevented the firm's management from solving a problem, but it also eliminated its ability to develop an opportunity.

The First Virtue:
Weight Forward On Skis

"The best way out is always through."

–Robert Frost

IN PRACTICING THE FIRST VIRTUE, managers use the beginning-skier instinct as a behavioral trigger to do the *opposite*. This means that when instinct says to avoid, delay, put off, or let someone else handle the issue, you should treat this feeling as a signal to confront and resolve it.

Most employment attorneys would have to find another way to make a living if supervisors managed like good skiers. Weight-forward management is powerful yet rare. Understanding and using this technique will lead you to dramatically improve your management style and results. The next time the warning light goes on and you start to lean away, make this impulse a trigger to do the opposite. You cannot make problems with your Kevins and Marys go away by avoiding them or pretending they don't exist. Instead of protecting you from the legal system, inaction will more likely deposit you there.

Weight Forward in the Workplace
Despite her inauspicious beginning on the ski slope, Sally's instructor taught her to do something so counterintuitive that it first seemed preposterous. When instinct urged her to lean back and get her weight closer to the uphill slope, he instructed her to do the opposite—bend her knees and put her weight forward on her skis. Though it took many repeti-

tions, Sally began to catch on by week's end. She discovered she could control speed and direction by going exactly contrary to instinct.

Following her return to work, Sally was struck by the parallel between the instinct she had overcome when learning to ski and the instinct that encouraged her to avoid confronting Kevin and Mary.

Sally pondered, "What if every time I feel this instinct to avoid, I treat it as a signal to do the opposite? Instead of thinking, 'This is a hassle I'll deal with later,' I'll say to myself, 'Weight forward!'"

Sally began by scheduling a meeting with Kevin to address her expectations of a respectful, professional office environment. Then she resolved to help Mary raise her performance and attendance to acceptable levels—without being deterred by Mary's passive resistance or Sally's own fear of a legal claim. Sally met with Mary and outlined the gaps that needed to be closed. She also resolved to monitor progress and have follow-up meetings with both Mary and Kevin.

As Sally became more comfortable keeping her weight forward in the workplace, she used the same proactive approach to pursue opportunities for improvement. Employees began to notice the difference. Productivity, morale, and teamwork went up. Sally happily discovered that addressing issues promptly meant less time fixing things and more time building things.

Managers, like skiers, can be intimidated by new difficulties regardless of their experience or skill. Sally occasionally experienced a return of the avoidance instinct. However, just as on the slopes, Sally learned to counter the instinct and put her weight forward.

Tools and Techniques

For the workplace skier, here are four tips.

✔ **Tip 1:** Ski the entire run,
especially in investigations.

Management sometimes begins the ski run by putting weight forward, owning responsibility, and proactively confronting workplace challenges or pursuing opportunities. However, many positive beginnings come to naught because management fails to follow through to bring the matter to an appropriate conclusion. To avoid legal actions, it is especially crucial to ski the entire run in conducting internal investigations.

Stopping Short

After receiving a complaint of sexual harassment at an out-of-state office, the HR director promptly flew there and investigated. The offending employee essentially admitted the complainant's allegations but asserted he had not known his conduct caused offense. The HR director and local office manager issued a written reprimand and warning based on his conduct. The employee apologized and ceased further conduct of a sexual nature. The complainant accepted the apology. Concluding that the matter had been resolved successfully, the HR director flew home.

All was not well, however. Although the male worker ceased further sexual misconduct, he misguidedly attempted to make his colleague feel more comfortable by keeping his distance. She interpreted this distance as resentment and gave him similar space. Silently, the division grew. The office manager sensed the problem but, fearing the female employee's "militancy," did not address it. Eventually, a seemingly innocuous exchange between the coworkers broke into open conflict. The female employee stormed out of the office and did not return. Instead, she hired a lawyer and brought claims of sexual harassment and retaliation.

What went wrong? The employer got off to an excellent start. The HR director quickly conducted an investigation and formulated, communicated, and executed a sound corrective-action plan.

However, in cases involving internal harassment complaints, the run is not skied until all parties are reintegrated into a positive working environment. Apologies and promises to behave differently are important, but they may not be sufficient when wounds are fresh and the danger of misunderstandings or erroneous assumptions still exists. By leaving the parties to their own devices to resume a working relationship, the HR director and office manager undid their positive work. The HR director's to-do list lacked follow-up steps; meanwhile, the office manager gave in to the self-protective instinct to lean back. The HR director should have discussed with these employees how to resume their working relationship and resolve lingering concerns. And she should have established follow-up contact. The office manager should have intervened when he first saw the problem early on, before any real damage was done.

Completing the Run

A secretary struggled in her job. Her company had recently switched software programs and she was having great difficulty making the transition. Her frustration was mirrored by her boss, who depended on her work. Eventually, she quit and filed for unemployment. The HR department opposed her application for benefits on the ground that she left voluntarily. She responded by asserting that she left for good cause—to escape sexual harassment. This was the first the employer heard of the alleged problem.

After receiving this information, the general manager (GM) had some decisions to make. Should he continue to contest the unemployment claim because the employee never notified the company of the alleged problem? Or, should the company quietly back away from the proceeding and cross its fingers in hopes that the former employee would not eventually move on to a different forum where the stakes would be much higher?

Ultimately, the GM did neither. He conducted an internal investigation as if the secretary were still employed. He telephoned the former employee, expressed concern about potential problems in the work environment, and asked for information so that he could conduct an investigation. He learned that several staff members, including a couple of supervisors, had engaged in joking and teasing of a sexual nature. Although no one had ever complained, the GM determined that this conduct was inconsistent with company policy and values. As a result, he reprimanded the supervisors and arranged for anti-harassment training.

The GM then contacted the former employee again, explained what had been done, and apologized if she had been offended or felt uncomfortable in the workplace. He also explained that the company would not contest her application for unemployment benefits. The GM's staff predicted that he was, in effect, inviting her to sue for sexual harassment. However, the former employee thanked him for his attention to her concerns and did not file a sexual harassment claim. Further, she subsequently played a pivotal role in avoiding another disgruntled employee's sexual harassment claim; on the company's behalf, she submitted an affidavit that persuaded the Equal Employment Opportunity Commission to find in the company's favor and dissuaded the other ex-employee and her attorney from going forward.

✓ **Tip 2:** Lean forward to prevent workplace violence.

Studies of preventable workplace violence often reveal ignored warning signs and tensions that built to the breaking point. Just as the fear of workplace litigation tends to increase the likelihood of its occurrence, so too does the fear of violence tend to increase the risk as it encourages leaning back on skis and giving the problem a wide berth. Yet experts recommend putting your weight forward. Dennis A. Davis, author of *Threats Pending Fuses Burning: Managing Workplace Violence*, advises employers that if conditions exist indicating the potential for violence, "address them immediately!"

The Link between Unemployment Claims and Litigation

Decisions on unemployment-benefits claims usually have no binding effect on subsequent legal proceedings, such as discrimination claims, and the decisions may not even be admissible. Also, the stakes are much lower than in litigation. Nevertheless, high-stakes employment litigation sometimes originates in unemployment proceedings, where employees first begin to express their brainlock and allege unlawful treatment, and where someone in the unemployment agency points them in the direction of the EEOC or to a plaintiff's attorney.

Especially when the potential for harassment, discrimination, wrongful discharge, or other legal claims exists, you should put weight forward on skis at the outset of an unemployment claim. Decide clearly and deliberately whether to contest the claim or not. If you do contest it, take the proceeding very seriously despite the relatively low stakes. Make sure everything submitted or presented to the unemployment agency is consistent, supportable, and non-inflammatory. (For example, just because you fired an employee for reasons A and B, do not pile on with reasons C through Z.) Even when the unemployment proceeding seems like the bunny hill, it can lead to a much steeper and scarier slope. Thus, if the potential for litigation exists— such as when the employee has previously made threats, there are potential contract issues, or there are marked differences in age, gender, race, or other protected classifications—seek the advice of your employment counsel before you respond to the agency.

Researchers have developed various profiles of characteristics that indicate an individual with an unusually high risk of workplace violence. These include: (a) showing contempt for authority; (b) blaming others excessively; (c) viewing change as a personal attack; (d) holding grudges; (e) making threats, subtle or overt; (f) intimidating or harassing others; (g) having alcohol, drug, or other significant problems outside work; (h) owning and talking about weapons; (i) speaking of others in dehumanizing terms; (j) spreading lies; (k) swearing excessively or using sexually explicit language; (l) arguing frequently and intensely; and (m) having committed violent acts in the past and talking about them.

Reflect for a moment on these characteristics and then ask yourself: aren't such employees the very ones you want to avoid at all costs? You probably want to lean away as far as possible. Yet when you do, the problem festers, builds in intensity, and grows to such dimensions that it may ultimately be expressed with violence.

It's important to note that profiles and profile characteristics are generalizations. They are not predictors in every situation or for every employee. And, as the story of the food-processing company discussed earlier shows, violence doesn't always come from the profile—just as lawsuits don't always come from the litigation-prone.

When you put your weight forward on this admittedly challenging ski run, you recognize that inaction is one of the worst options. Instead of avoiding, formulate and carry out a game plan to defuse the threat by consulting HR and security personnel, employment counsel, and, depending on the circumstances, law enforcement and the company's employee assistance program. The game plan will vary from situation to situation. However, one lesson emerges clearly: when warning signs appear, refuse to allow the situation to continue. Get help and take prompt corrective action.

✓ **Tip 3:** Keep weight forward during
the initial employment period.

Many employers have policies establishing initial employment periods in which they assess the fit of new employees. However, most employers don't use these policies effectively. They would be well served by learning from the following story.

The new CEO of a struggling long-distance telephone company turned its fortunes around by creating a weight-forward culture in his organization. A key step was to adopt a policy establishing a sixty-day initial review period for new hires to determine if the fit was right. If signs arose that the new hire would not be able to meet expectations, action was taken. The company held managers and supervisors accountable for how effectively they used this policy and whether they overlooked warning signs that later ripened into major problems. This proactive approach not only paid off in weeding out misfits quickly, but it also impressed on employees and supervisors the necessity of meeting expectations and being productive—lessons that continued long after the sixty-day mark. During this CEO's tenure, the company posted fifteen consecutive years of increasing profitability.

The company's assertiveness in terminating poor hires would seem to make it an excellent candidate for employment litigation. Ironically, the contrary was true. Hundreds of terminations over the years produced no claims. The company's weight-forward approach let employees know where they stood and promoted consistent treatment. Instead of succumbing to the instinct to avoid (often out of a fear of potential legal trouble), this employer made it a practice to confront employee problems at the earliest opportunity and solve them either by helping the employee make the necessary corrections or by recognizing that the employee needed to work elsewhere. As a result, neither brainlock nor grounds for suit arose.

✔ **Tip 4:** Use weight-forward to become
a workplace star.

As the story of the telephone company shows, a weight-forward approach to management not only prevents claims but also helps the organization in many other ways. Another illustration of this point comes from Robert E. Kelley, adjunct professor of business at Carnegie Mellon University, who conducted research into creating a profile of a workplace standout. As Kelley recounts in his book *How to Be a Star at Work*, his research team identified acknowledged workplace stars, examined them for common characteristics, and then compared the characteristics to those of a group of average performers. To Kelley's chagrin, no statistically significant differences emerged. So the team shadowed both stars and average performers at work to observe what they actually did, as opposed to characteristics they possessed. Of the nine key differences that emerged, Kelley lists initiative first. Stars stood

---

Legal Nugget

"Probationary Period" Problems

The legal system has occasionally laid traps for well-intentioned employers with policies establishing initial or introductory employment periods. When employers have called them "probationary periods" or failed to specify that after the introductory period, employment remains "at will," terminated employees have sued for wrongful discharge alleging an implied contract that once they got past the initial employment period, they would not be terminated except for cause. Thus, even though policies establishing introductory employment periods can constitute useful tools for employers, you must use caution. Don't call it a "probationary period" since this may imply tenure thereafter. The policy should expressly state that employees remain employed at-will even after they successfully complete the initial employment period. The following is an example:

> Introductory Employment Period
>
> The first ninety-day period of a new employee's employment is designed to provide training and orientation to familiarize the employee with job duties and expectations. It also provides an opportunity for both employee and management to determine if the Company is the right place for the employee to work. Either the employee or management may decide that the fit is not right and end the employment relationship at that time. If, however, employment continues past the introductory period, it remains "at will," meaning either the employee or the Company may terminate the relationship at any time for any reason with or without cause or advance notice.

---

out not because of their IQ, education, interpersonal skills, or creativity but because they regularly took initiative. They saw problems not as hassles to avoid but challenges to meet. Stars were not afraid to take risks or step outside their job descriptions if the company's interests called for it. Whether required to or not, they helped others.

Initiative is another way of saying "weight forward"—and mastering this technique can help you become a management star.

In Conclusion

There may be wisdom in the adage to trust your instincts. However, this adage will not work for you with employment issues until you have mastered the habit of keeping your weight forward on skis. Now is the time to translate the avoidance instinct into a message to apply energy, initiative, and gumption. In other words, it's time to ski the entire run.

Chapter One Highlights

The First Sin: Managing Like a Beginning Skier

The self-protective instinct tells managers to lean away or avoid confronting employee problems, but this reaction makes the situation worse.

☛ The fear of employment litigation leads to inaction that increases the risk of its occurrence.

☛ Employee problems are often opportunities in disguise; yet the fear of uncertainty stops you from pursuing opportunities.

The First Virtue: Weight Forward on Skis

☛ Managers control speed and direction in the workplace by doing the opposite of what instinct commands. Instead of avoiding worrisome employee challenges, confront them.

☛ Managers must ski the entire run. Follow up and follow through to make sure the plan has been fully and properly implemented.

☛ Fear of violence produces a strong tendency to lean back on skis. Yet there is never a more important time to do the opposite. When you spot conditions indicating the potential for workplace violence, get help and develop a game plan immediately.

☛ A weight-forward policy regarding new hires compels supervisors to make early evaluations regarding the fit between a new employee and a position, and holds supervisors accountable for their evaluations. This approach weeds out misfits quickly, underscores the importance of productivity, and decreases the potential for wrongful-discharge litigation.

☛ Workplace stars continually demonstrate initiative. One way to become a management star is to be alert for the beginning-skier instinct and use it to trigger the opposite behavior.

CHAPTER 2

The Second Sin:
Dissin' Your Employees

"The thousand injuries of Fortunato I had borne as I best could, but when he ventured upon insult, I vowed revenge."

—Edgar Allan Poe, *The Cask of Amontillado*

THE SIN OF DISSIN' MEANS DISRESPECTING an employee. It means engaging in the kind of insulting or demeaning behavior that causes brainlock, making workers so upset that they cannot move forward emotionally or psychologically without striking back. However, this type of dissin' does not typically stem from managerial conduct intended to be humiliating or demeaning. Rather, it's the *unintentional* insult that causes the trouble. One culprit? The manager's instinct to avoid.

Executive Sabotage Follows a Layoff

As part of a corporate reorganization, a company terminated a long-term senior executive. The company handled all layoffs in the same way. As a result, an HR staff member, well below the director level, went with a company security guard to the executive's office to tell him the decision and direct him to box up his things immediately. Afterward the guard escorted him through the halls past other employees, followed him to the company parking lot, and watched him drive away.

Not long thereafter, the company's president received an anonymous note stating, "How dare you treat me this way. You had your kitchen staff box up my things and walk me out of here like a common criminal. You will pay for your insensitivity!" A private investigator subsequently traced the note to the former executive.

This ex-employee did make the company pay—with interest. Although his computer password had been deleted at the time of termination, the ex-executive knew a colleague's password. Through it, he accessed the company's computers and deleted critical business information. The company estimated the damage at more than $20 million. Moreover, the company had been scheduled to go public with a stock offering. The invasion of its computer system scotched this plan.

This story illustrates how powerfully the feeling of indignity serves as a motivator for destructive action. The ex-executive was no doubt deeply pained by the loss of his job. However, as Edgar Allan Poe understood, it was not this loss but the humiliating way the company carried it out that prompted him to wreak havoc on his former employer's computer system.

A study of employee discharges in Ohio in the late 1990s focused on the manner in which employees were terminated, as opposed to the reasons. Employees were asked if the employer treated them with respect—regardless of the reason for termination or whether employees agreed with it. Of employees who said they were terminated in a dignified manner, less than one-half of 1 percent went on to sue their former employers. Employees who said their employers did not terminate them in a respectful manner were over *thirty-five times more likely* to file claims.

The solution therefore seems simple. If you have to inflict injury, do it without insult. Unfortunately, however, the solution is not nearly as easy as it sounds. You must eliminate not only the intentional insult but the unwitting one. Eliminating the former requires self-control. Eliminating the latter requires an understanding of human nature and your own instinct to avoid.

Delegating a Termination Leads to Violence and Litigation

A construction company superintendent decided to terminate an employee for poor attendance. However, because the superintendent needed to attend a funeral, he delegated responsibility for carrying out the decision to a lower-level supervisor. Anxious about the potential reaction of a burly construction worker, the deputized supervisor carried out the discharge but indicated that the decision was not his. The employee took the news calmly. Two days later, however, he returned to the work site to accost the superintendent, knocking him to the ground with a blow to the face followed by kicks in the side that broke ribs. While being pulled off his victim, the ex-employee raged that the superintendent was "not man enough to tell me to my face!" His anger still not quenched (and undeterred by a guilty plea to assault and battery), the employee subsequently sued the company for race and national-origin discrimination.

The beginning-skier instinct continually urges you to postpone, to wait and see, or to create space or distance between you and your employees. When observing something you don't like or that makes you uneasy, the natural tendency is to hold off until you're forced to take action. Typically, however, when you finally do take action, a great deal of momentum has been generated in the wrong direction. Thus, the corrective measures you employ require a great deal more time and energy, generate less satisfying results, and are more likely to inflict the unwitting insult. Moreover, because of your discomfort, it may be tempting to use someone else (or e-mail or voicemail) to avoid face-to-face encounters—even though the more sensitive the message, the greater the disrespect if you fail to convey it in person. Like the construction superintendent, managers continue to learn this lesson the hard way.

E-mails Exacerbate a Soured Relationship

After a start-up tech company began to grow, the CEO hired a talented Harvard MBA to be CFO. Unfortunately, the relationship soured within a few months and ended unhappily. E-mail played a critical role. The understandable and often healthy tension in a relationship between a fiscally conservative CFO and an entrepreneurial CEO was greatly exacerbated by their use of e-mail as their primary means of communication—even though their offices were only three doors apart.

The endless e-mail strings led to a breakdown in trust and understanding, with neither party investing in face time to resolve issues and create synergy with their different areas of strength. Their dashed-off messages—reply and counter, reply and counter—took on increasingly harsh and defensive tones. Yet neither executive would walk five yards down the hall for a face-to-face discussion. Finally, an e-mail informed the CFO that since he evidently questioned the CEO's ethics and competence, he needed to start looking for another job "now!" The relationship ended. Brainlock had set in, followed by legal wrangling over the terms of the CFO's executive employment agreement.

An Executive Uses the Gunnysack

Supervisors who manage like beginning skiers often use the "gunnysack" approach. When they observe something in an employee's conduct, performance, or attendance that is less than satisfying, they don't confront the employee. Instead, they make a mental note of the deficiency and save it for later, like picking up an acorn and putting it in the gunnysack for later consumption or use. When they do this, they frequently have experiences such as the following one.

The executive director of a nonprofit association was excited about a programming manager she had just hired. Her excitement soon dimmed, however. Although managers were given a lot of discretion over the hours they worked, she could not help noticing that the programming manager typically came in well after other employees and was one of the first to leave. Nevertheless, the director said nothing, reasoning that after the manager developed a better appreciation for the scope of his job, his time commitment would increase.

The work pattern did not change. Even worse, the manager turned in written reports late, incomplete, and filled with

---

The D-I-S Method, Diversity, and Employment Discrimination

Although employment discrimination cases can be proved by direct evidence—for example, by statements from a decision maker that the employee's protected class status (race, color, gender, religion, disability, age, or national origin) motivated an adverse employment action—the vast majority of cases turn on indirect evidence. Claims of employment discrimination are typically fought over whether one can *infer* from circumstances that race, gender, etc., played a role in the employer's decision. Employees draw inferences from employer conduct (most notably the types of inconsistency described in Chapter Five), which they assert proves more likely than not that management harbored a discriminatory motive for its action.

What starts employees on the road to inferring discriminatory animus? Management's failure to D-I-S its employees, using the Direct, Immediate, and Specific communication outlined in the next section. Employees make assumptions to fill in gaps in a manager's communications. When the white male supervisor fails to D-I-S his black female subordinate, it is almost inevitable that she will infer from his faulty communication that race and gender are at the heart of the matter. Thus, when you develop the habit of D-I-S'ng all employees, you eliminate both the communication gaps and the disrespect that so often combine to produce Title VII litigation when supervisor and employee differ by race, gender, or other protected classification. Indeed, there is perhaps no better way to make diversity a source of synergy—as opposed to conflict or mistrust—than for you to make a commitment to using the D-I-S method of communication with your employees.

---

errors. Programs he was scheduled to begin had to be delayed, although he always had explanations. The executive director hinted at her displeasure on several occasions but avoided confronting the programming manager directly. Instead, each negative observation became an acorn she picked up and put in her gunnysack.

As the director continued to observe the gap between what she thought she had hired and what she got, the gunnysack grew difficult to lug around. Finally one day, when the programming manager arrived at 10:30 a.m. without a report that had been due the day before, the executive director dumped out the acorns. She erupted, acidly reciting the myriad problems of the previous six months. The programming manager responded with a litany of the obstacles he faced and protested that it was unfair to blame him for problems he could not control and issues she had never raised. By the end of the meeting, their relationship was permanently damaged. Brainlock and a trip to the legal system soon followed. An earlier chat with the director about their respective religious traditions led the programming manager to assert that he was a victim of discrimination based on both religion and gender.

The Second Virtue:
D-I-S'ng Your Employees

"If it were done when 'tis done, then 'twere well it were done quickly."

—William Shakespeare, *Macbeth*

THE BEST WAY TO COUNTER NEGATIVE DISSIN' is with a technique that sounds the same but means something very different. It is called D-I-S and stands for Direct, Immediate, and Specific communication with employees. This type of D-I-S avoids unintentional insults and allows management to inflict "injury" without causing brainlock. Even more important, this type of D-I-S serves as a positive communication tool for reinforcing behavior the employer wants to see repeated.

The Little GM Uses Big D-I-S

A company that sold oxygen in heavy cylindrical containers employed a number of burly men to load, unload, store, fill, and deliver the cylinders to customers. The work was arduous. The laborers typically lacked high school diplomas. A couple of them were ex-cons, complete with bulging muscles and tattoos.

By contrast, the company's general manager was female, probably not over five feet three, and weighed 120 pounds. Recipe for disaster? Custer at the Little Big Horn? Hardly. In the years this diminutive GM ran the facility, there were a couple of incidents of intimidation and one ugly confrontation that necessitated a 911 call. However, none of these involved the GM directly. She more than held her ground, and not by threats, curses, or histrionics. Instead, she made it a practice to address issues without hesitation by looking employees directly in the eye and telling them specifically what she liked or did not like. In fact, she did not even find managing such a workforce stressful. "Look," she explained, "they know where I stand, and I let them know where they stand."

The Benefits of Virtuous Managing

Employees who get D-I-S'd don't feel insulted. They feel they know where they stand and have received an opportunity to be successful. Managers who practice the D-I-S method promote agreement and understanding. By communicating directly, without delay and with specific information about what they expect, they quickly correct erroneous assumptions and convey their message in a manner that promotes willingness to follow their lead. But the D-I-S method works even when employees remain unpersuaded that the manager's decision is correct. Instead of resisting, passively or aggressively, employees who feel respected are unlikely to develop brainlock over decisions with which they disagree.

Although it's possible to D-I-S someone and be harsh or undiplomatic, if used properly, the method will consistently produce constructive communication with employees regarding expected performance, conduct, and attendance. Experience has shown that managers who D-I-S their employees demonstrate greater sensitivity, diplomacy, and understanding, yet at the same time, they effectively let their employees know where they stand. They don't let their frus-

The D-I-S Method and Harassment Prevention

Conventional anti-harassment policies and training programs exhort victims not to put up with offensive or harassing conduct and to take their complaints to HR or management. That is absolutely the correct message. However, to help ensure a legally compliant, professional working environment, the employer's preventive efforts should take into account two important but usually overlooked realities of workplace harassment: (1) many if not most "harassers" do not think their behavior is unwelcome or offensive; and (2) many if not most victims are extremely reluctant to take any remedial action, no matter how proactive the employer's policies and training programs.

Hence the value of the D-I-S method. In most situations, if the offended party D-I-S'd the offending party—told him directly, immediately, and specifically that the behavior caused discomfort and needed to stop—the problem would end right there without resentment, hostility, or retaliation. Why? First, because the harasser was not knowingly or intentionally causing offense but was making erroneous assumptions about what was welcome. And, second, because no pattern of behavior had set in which the harasser interpreted acquiescence as encouragement and then felt unfairly surprised by a subsequent accusation that he had been causing offense all along.

Because of its utility, the D-I-S method should be included in anti-harassment training programs and policies as an option for dealing with offensive workplace conduct. Keep in mind that for legal reasons, company policy, management, and HR can never *require* that employees attempt self-help (such as D-I-S'ng the offender) or state or imply that such action is a precondition for seeking help from the employer. Also, if management or HR becomes aware of a problem that an employee has attempted to solve through self-help, it *must* ski the run by following up to make sure that the self-help worked and that no further action needs to be taken.

tration build to the point where it interferes with their ability to communicate. In contrast to numerous managers in today's litigious world, they actually feel good about supervising a workforce and positive about their relationship with their employees.

Tools and Techniques

To get the most out of the D-I-S method of communication, here are three useful tips:

✔ Tip 1: Make sure you're truly specific.

Often the most effective way to manage without appearing to be harsh or punitive is to get specific. You are more likely to insult employees when you use a label of some sort to characterize them or what they have done.

When managers use general words, descriptions, or labels, it's typically not to insult employees. Rather, it's because the general is easier than the specific. The former requires less effort and preparation. For example, if you say an employee has a "bad attitude," you know what you mean. But will the employee? Or rather, will he reject this label and instead think you are the one with the attitude problem? The general label creates too much gray area, too much room for differing perceptions.

To avoid the label or perception problem, your communication to the employee should be preceded by asking yourself questions such as, "Precisely what behavior bothers me about this employee?" and "What are some specific examples of the problem, including names, places, dates, and outcomes?" Instead of thinking about employee performance in terms of "sub-par," "poor," or "unacceptable," ask yourself, "In what specific ways have their efforts fallen short?" and "Precisely what results did the employee fail to obtain and what are the consequences?" and "What are the specific measuring sticks I can use to distinguish success from failure?"

Your answers to these questions form the basis of your subsequent communications with your employees. Once you shed labels and get specific about what needs to happen, by when, and why it's so important, you will invariably report progress. But the technique takes practice. Beware the tendency to start specific and end general. For example, don't bring up a specific project involving a specific objective during a specific time frame and then say the effort "stunk." Instead, point out specifically how the project fell short and what the consequences were: "Sarah, we agreed in our meeting on October 12th that you were to complete the twelve-month budget for the new product launch by December 15th so that we could meet with the bank on our financing request prior to the holidays. You submitted the budget on December 22nd without projections on the anticipated costs of obtaining patents, trademarks, and copyright protection. This has resulted in at least one month of delay, increased our costs, potentially hurt our credibility with the bank, and helped our competitors."

Engineering Improvement in an Engineer's Behavior

The head of engineering confronted one of his engineers about her performance and the friction she had generated with fellow engineers. She denied having problems with her performance or how she treated others. Instead, she said the problem was that both he and the other engineers were male and no doubt were uncomfortable working with a woman. When asked to recount his communications with her about the problems, the manager used phrases such as, "Your engineering work is not as good as the others'," "I'm not sure your engineering skills are up to par," and "I think you have a bad attitude." These general labels were rapidly leading to brainlock and a gender-discrimination claim.

So the manager committed to ditch the generalizations. Instead he identified as precisely as possible the gap between her engineering work and his expectations, including potential corrective measures, training needed, and other resources that might enable her to close the gap. With respect to attitude, he identified specific instances of unacceptable behavior, including actual words used, tone, volume, and e-mail messages showing that she treated coworkers inappropriately.

Equipped with this information, he met with her and spoke specifically about the gaps that needed to be closed and possible ways to do so. The steps included changes the female engineer needed to make as well as changes he needed to make to clarify the path to acceptable performance and develop a stronger team spirit among his engineers. The manager reported an immediate improvement in her responsiveness once he got away from general labels or descriptions and got precise about what needed to happen. He no longer needed legal advice about fending off a potential gender discrimination claim. Instead, he had helped to develop a productive employee.

✓ **Tip 2:** D-I-S
     the positives.

So far, the focus of D-I-S has primarily been on solving problems. However, many managers believe that the best way to use the tool is to reinforce the positive things employees do. When you let employees know directly, immediately, and specifically about something beneficial, you simultaneously increase the likelihood of experiencing such behavior in the future and decrease the likelihood of having future problems to D-I-S.

A study of employee recognition identified three types: (a) formal, such as the annual black-tie dinner; (b) informal, such as an employee-of-the-month parking space, picture on the wall, or feature in the company newsletter; and (c) direct acknowledgment by an employee's immediate supervisor. Researchers surveyed employees in a number of different industries and geographic locations to ask (1) Which of the three types have you witnessed or experienced most frequently? and (2) Which is most valuable?

In response to question (1), employees stated that they had experienced or observed formal recognition most frequently and direct recognition least frequently. Their responses to question (2) were reversed; they valued direct recognition the most and formal recognition the least. In other words, what they desired most they experienced least.

Unfortunately, in the twenty years since Spencer Johnson and Ken Blanchard advised us in *The One Minute Manager* "to catch employees doing something right," the advice has rarely been heeded. Yet the value of an immediate supervisor's praise for a specific action cannot be overstated. It not only helps cement loyalty and good will, but it also increases the likelihood that the positive act will be repeated on a more beneficial scale. As reported by Bob Nelson in *1001 Ways to Reward Employees*, a boss's personal recognition of a specific act or behavior is a more powerful motivator than traditional items, including money. Most employees want to be successful and want to please their boss. They will work a seventy-hour week if they think it means something to their boss and their company. They may feel insulted if you recognize them with a modest gift certificate as payment for their effort, but they will feel rewarded if you thank them.

Because visual images or symbols can prompt behavior, consider using a colorful or good-sized battery as a paperweight on your desk to remind you about the importance of D-I-S'ng. A battery generates energy and has two terminals, positive and negative. Visualize plugging a battery into the D-I-S method to energize it and ensure it gets applied to both negative and positive behavior. Just as your recognition of your employees' positive acts will produce repetition and enhancement, recognizing the benefits of the D-I-S method and using the battery will help you repeat and enhance your most effective communications.

The Author Practices What He Preaches

My receptionist, "Gloria," was an efficient, well-organized woman in her 50s who had worked for many years in the armed forces. Although she was highly competent and kept excellent track of the office and her boss, Gloria's communication style lacked warmth. She took a no-nonsense, state-your-business, don't-waste-my-time approach to interpersonal communications.

One day, she patched in a telephone call to me from one of my clients, "Bill." Seeming pleasantly surprised, Bill mentioned that Gloria had been friendly on the telephone. Immediately afterward, I walked out to the reception area and told Gloria I had just spoken with Bill. She replied crisply that she already knew this, since she had handled the call in the first place. (As you can tell, she *was* no-nonsense). Undeterred, I shared Bill's comment about his pleasure at her friendliness on the telephone. Gloria said nothing, but I could detect a slight blush. Thereafter, I observed a touch of warmth and friendliness that had not existed before when she answered the telephone.

As this story illustrates, one of the beauties of D-I-S'ng the positives is that the boss can produce improvement without having to order it, request it, pay for it, or even plead for it. Many managers have reported similar results after experimenting with using the D-I-S method for praise. When they went to an employee personally (directly), just after something positive had occurred (immediately), and described what the employee had done and why it was good (specifically), the employee inevitably tended to do more of the same in the future.

✓ **Tip 3:** D-I-S in writing:
  "List, Meet, Write."

Abraham Lincoln once said that for important messages, he liked to communicate through two senses: hearing and sight. His dictum holds true for the D-I-S method. It has more impact when you do it both orally and in writing.

One of the easiest and most effective D-I-S tools is the follow-up note, memo, or e-mail. As a rule of thumb, it should be no longer than a page and given no more than a day after you D-I-S the employee orally. The note should simply summarize what you just communicated: "Pat, this note follows our conversation this morning. Your staying late last evening to analyze the Acme Tool account allowed us to solve the problem first thing in the morning before the customer could get worked up about it. Thank you."

Even if the D-I-S message is not praise, the written word will make it more effective (and help protect you from litigation). "Terry, this memo follows our meeting this morning in which I described a problem I have observed. Despite our discussion of the necessity that you be here at 8:00 a.m. to cover the phones since customers start calling at that hour, in the past two weeks you came in ten minutes late one day and fifteen minutes late another. As I explained, this cannot continue. In our meeting, you committed to meeting our attendance standard. This is what I expect. If you have any questions or if this memo does not accurately summarize our discussion, please see me immediately."

A good way to add the written word to your management toolbox is to follow the three-step process called "List, Meet, Write." Let's say you need to have an important discussion with one of your employees regarding: (a) a disciplinary issue; (b) new duties and responsibilities; or (c) a major corporate change that will impact her job status. In order to maintain control and direction in the conversation, yet have the freedom to listen (see Chapter Seven), you make a List of the important points to cover. You then Meet with the employee and make sure you cover all points. Within a day, you Write a one-page follow-up memo, letter, or e-mail to the employee summarizing the conversation. Make this a practice and watch your effectiveness as a communicator rise to all-star level!

The Tough Texan Takes to Writing

The barrel-chested construction manager from Texas attended a training program on the D-I-S method, including the steps for putting it into writing. He found that it confirmed many of his own convictions and practices. Later, he sought legal blessing on terminating an employee in several legally protected classes. He proudly exclaimed that he'd repeatedly and properly D-I-S'd the employee so there should be no unpleasant surprises. A review of the file, however, revealed a complete lack of documentation. When confronted with this fact, and the problems it presented for the employer to go through with the termination, the Texan shook his head and said, "Hell, I don't have a problem telling anyone to their face what's what, but when it comes to writing things down, it just ain't my style!"

Nevertheless, this manager soon learned that even he could master the short follow-up memo to an employee on an important subject. In fact, he mastered it so well that eventually he became an internal trainer for his company on the D-I-S method of communication, including its written forms.

Chapter Two Highlights

The Second Sin: Dissin' Your Employees

☛ Typically, the insult rather than the injury produces brainlock and the desire to strike back through the legal system or otherwise.

☛ Regardless of the reason for termination, discharged employees are at least thirty-five times more likely to sue the employer if they feel the manner of termination did not respect their dignity.

☛ Most managerial insults are unintentional.

☛ You unwittingly dis your employees by letting the instinct to avoid influence your behavior:
   - You avoid face-to-face confrontations when you need them most.
   - You use e-mail or other distancing forms of communication to convey sensitive messages that you should convey in person.
   - You treat employee problems like acorns that you pick up and put in a gunnysack. When the gunnysack becomes too heavy to carry, you dump the acorns on the employee.

The Second Virtue: D-I-S'ng Your Employees

☛ Make your communications Direct, Immediate, and Specific.

☛ The D-I-S method promotes agreement or consensus between you and your employees.

☛ Even when employees disagree with your decision, they are more likely to accept it if you use the D-I-S method.

☛ Include the D-I-S method in your anti-harassment training program and policy.

☛ Get specific. Instead of using labels such as "bad attitude" or "poor performance," zero in on the precise gap between your expectations and the employee's performance, conduct, or attendance. Then communicate using these precise descriptions.

☛ D-I-S the positives. Direct, immediate, and specific recognition of behavior you like will ensure that it will be repeated and enhanced. Use a battery to remind you to use the method for both the positives and the negatives.

☛ D-I-S in writing. In a page or less, and in a day or less, follow up an oral D-I-S with a written summary of the important points you already made to the employee. Use the "List, Meet, Write" technique.

☛ D-I-S'ng enables you to supervise a diverse workforce without risking that employees will fill communication voids with assumptions that racial, gender, or other protected-class differences are involved.

CHAPTER 3

The Third Sin:
Rationalizing Away Truth

"Oh what a tangled web we weave, when first we practice to deceive!"

—Sir Walter Scott

THE SIN OF RATIONALIZING AWAY TRUTH grows out of the self-protective instinct, like the tendency to lean back on one's skis. Honesty has a way of bringing issues to the surface and intensifying relationships. Thus, when instinct dictates avoiding a difficult issue, the natural thought is that in this case honesty is not the best policy—and when a person of integrity needs reasons for avoiding honesty, rationalization supplies them. Logic provides plausible arguments for saying or doing something that the gut says is not right.

A Well-Intentioned Lie Produces Ugly Results

After many years in business, "George," the owner of a staffing company, decided to retire. The company had offices in two states managed by able employees. One was easy-going; the other, named "Paul," was emotional and extremely profit-driven. George explained to the easy-going manager that he would only sell if both managers received substantial economic rewards and increased incomes. But he feared how Paul might react and so kept him in the dark. In fact, when Paul asked if George was selling, he replied, "Not at this time"—rationalizing that the prospectus had not yet been completed so technically speaking the company was not for sale.

Within a few months, George had a pending sale that would net him several million dollars while providing lucrative retention bonuses and increased salaries for his site managers. Three business days before the sale was scheduled to close, the buyer's representatives insisted on meeting Paul, of whom they had heard much. Nervously, George flew to the site to bring Paul to the home office for a meeting. When George informed Paul of the pending sale, the latter exploded in anger. Earnest explanations about financial rewards fell on deaf ears.

When Paul met the buyer's representatives, he let loose a stream of complaints, demands, and threats about what he could do if he decided to become a competitor. As a result, instead of handing the owner a multimillion-dollar check, the buyer pulled out. George fired Paul. Lawyers jumped into the fray as Paul asserted a wrongful discharge claim based on a written employment agreement. In addition to dealing with litigation, George had to work longer hours than ever as he commuted interstate while attempting to shore up his business and find another buyer.

A vastly different outcome would have resulted had George not succumbed to the temptation to rationalize and conceal the truth. Although volatile, Paul had demonstrated his commitment to the company's best interests. Had George told the truth instead of the "white lie," Paul would not have sabotaged the deal; instead, he probably would have gone out and gotten an even better one! Instead, there were shattered dreams and a trip to the legal system.

Aesop's 2,600-year-old saying about honesty being the best policy is an empty cliché in many workplaces. Even managers of integrity act dishonestly while thinking they are doing the right thing. They take the safe course by checking off a performance evaluation as "acceptable" when the performance is not. They create a false impression by omitting information, such as when they tell an employee an issue is settled as far as they're concerned even though they know it has not been resolved with senior management. They put a spin on information, telling an employee that layoffs appear unlikely even though the facts do not justify such optimism.

Why do honest managers behave dishonestly? Their self-protective instinct causes them to rationalize that the truth, while generally desirable, would be better avoided in current circumstances. But these rationalizations seldom, if ever, prove sound. Employees want and need to know where they stand. A fundamental ingredient of a successful relationship is the belief that the supervisor will be honest. Conversely, one of the worst ways of dissin' employees is to make them suspect their supervisor is not being honest with them. Once George lied to Paul, the relationship was over. It did no good to tell the site manager that the sale of the business would produce lucrative benefits for him.

When you are tempted to engage in this third Sin, picture the word "rationalize" as a two-word contraction: *rational* + *lies*. Here are some of the most common rational lies:

We're laying you off, not firing you. Many managers succumb to the temptation to make a performance-based termination more palatable by calling it a layoff. Whether motivated by a desire to avoid conflict or to be nice, asserting such a false reason is not a good idea. If the predominant reason for discharge is performance—that is, you would not have terminated certain employees if not for your assessment of their performance—you should say so. Otherwise, the employees will not believe your euphemism and will resent being lied to, which is a great way to make them candidates for brainlock. Moreover, if brainlock produces an employment claim, the plaintiffs' attorneys will attack your credibility and alleged motivation by dwelling on the contradiction between the reason you gave the employees and your real reason. Then, if you quickly replace the "laid off" employee with a new hire, watch out for the discrimination claim if the two employees fall into different classifications, such as race, age, or gender!

Being honest does not mean presenting terminated employees with a bill of particulars detailing all their faults. It simply means avoiding the temptation to tell the sugar-coated lie.

We're terminating you because you're employed at-will. Even if the employment relationship is at-will—that is, set for no definite time period and capable of being terminated by either party with or without notice or cause—you must still be careful. There are many exceptions to this rule, including discrimination based on an employee's protected class status; retaliation for engaging in activity protected by state, local, or federal laws; and other statutory, constitutional, or judge-made exceptions to the at-will rule.

Management should never assert an employee's at-will status as a basis for termination. First of all, correct or not as a statement of law, it is dishonest. Unless your philosophy conforms to that of certain tyrannical Roman emperors, you don't fire employees for pleasure or simply because you can. You terminate them because their performance, conduct, or attendance is unacceptable or because you cannot economically justify their continued employment. The fact that they are at-will may insulate you from legal claims but does not serve as a predicate for action. Second, when you mask the real reason behind the at-will label, you invite the employee to speculate about the true causes for termination. As discussed in Chapter Six, such speculation produces only harm. Third, when you cite an employee's at-will status and your resulting freedom to make employment decisions as you see fit, you confirm in the fired employee's mind your cruelty and caprice. Brainlock will not be far away.

You earned a "satisfactory" on your performance evaluation. Perhaps the most common rationalized lie occurs when the supervisor rates performance, conduct, or attendance categories on an employee evaluation as acceptable when they are not. The rationalizations almost trip over themselves: "I didn't want to discourage her." "I was afraid he'd get angry if I marked the evaluation truthfully." "I thought the problem was temporary and he'd get over it." "I figured, gee, if I tell it like it is, we might get sued." Whatever the rationalization, by being dishonest, the supervisor allows a problem to continue uncorrected while dissin' the employee and creating optimal conditions for brainlock. The only real beneficiary of such rationalizations is a plaintiff's lawyer, who will use the phony evaluation to attack management's credibility. An employer would be better off shedding its entire performance evaluation system than to allow or encourage "false positives."

A Positive Evaluation Is Claimed to Be Retaliatory

After being disciplined by his female supervisor, an employee filed an internal claim alleging that she discriminated against him on the basis of gender. The organization resolved the claim by placing the employee under the direction of a new supervisor. Fearful of becoming the next target, this supervisor and successive supervisors continued to rate the employee's performance as "fully acceptable" over the next several years even though his performance clearly was not. The employee eventually filed a claim of unlawful retaliation in federal court based on these false, *positive* performance evaluations. If only his supervisors had been honest about his shortcomings, he claimed, he would have been placed in a remedial program through which he would have received training and turned his performance around. He thus would have overcome his shortcomings and earned promotions and higher pay. Therefore, he alleged, the false positive performance evaluations stunted his career growth.

A U.S. District Court *agreed* with him, ruling that such allegations could establish a claim of retaliation under Title VII of the Civil Rights Act of 1964. A federal appellate court ultimately disagreed with the lower court. Yet years of litigation and countless amounts of company time, money, and energy were wasted because a succession of supervisors gave an employee undeserved positive evaluations to avoid legal trouble. Even as the appellate court let the employer off the hook, it remarked that the employer's actions were indefensible as a matter of employment policy.

Maybe the truth isn't good enough. Managers' anxiety over whether they can justify a decision often induces them to embellish their reasons in order to make the action sound more supportable. If they fire an employee for a legitimate reason but worry about whether it is justification enough, they may add another reason or two—or six. The results: (a) brainlock as the employee obsesses on the false reasons while ignoring the legitimate ones, and (b) fodder for the legal system as the employee's lawyer exploits the false reasons to undermine management's ability to rely on the legitimate ones.

Dishonesty Has Tragic—and Legal—Consequences

A systems engineer suffered a severe head injury in a non-work-related automobile accident. Despite working diligently on rehabilitation, he suffered from ongoing limitations that kept him from performing to standard. His company fired him. Ultimately, the case went to court, where a federal court of appeals ruled that his superiors' actual reason for termination was their assessment of his inability to fulfill his job requirements. The court said that instead of being frank, the managers "lied to him by manufacturing reasons about his inability to get along with coworkers and clients" and by telling him they had intended to fire him even before his accident.

The engineer became so depressed that he threatened suicide and had to be hospitalized in a psychiatric unit. The court upheld an award of $200,000 under state law for his

---

Beware the Secret Recording

Although some states prohibit one person from secretly recording a conversation with another, federal law and most state laws follow the one-party consent rule. This means that if an employee secretly records a conversation with his boss, it is legal because the employee doing the taping "consents." Given the prevalence of the Third Sin of Mismanagement, it is not surprising that an increasing number of employees have been making surreptitious recordings of conversations with managers.

A 55-year-old dock worker claimed age discrimination after management cut his hours and denied him the opportunity to drive trucks. In fact, however, the dock supervisor, operations manager, and terminal manager all had compelling reasons for his treatment: (a) low productivity, (b) gross insubordination, and (c) threatening a coworker.

At an administrative hearing, the employee surprised management by playing tape recordings of conversations with all three managers. In those conversations, in response to persistent questioning from the employee, each manager expressly negated factors (a) through (c). In a hastily called recess with defense counsel, all three admitted lying to the employee. Why did they lie? (1) "He approached me at a particularly bad time when I was extremely busy... I didn't have time for a long debate." (2) "I know what a short fuse he has and I didn't want him to blow." (3) "I was afraid if I told him the truth, we might get sued." Avoiding the truth did not help avoid a lawsuit. Rather, it converted a slam-dunk defense into a substantial monetary settlement.

A good rule of thumb is to pretend that every conversation you have with an employee is being recorded. It may be!

---

emotional-distress claim and then awarded an additional $100,000 in back pay and compensatory damages under the Americans with Disabilities Act. The court held that the two awards were not duplicative since the ADA award focused on the termination itself, whereas the larger state-law award focused on the *dishonest manner of termination* and its impact on the employee's psyche. Perhaps to show its distaste for such dishonesty, the court upheld an additional award of attorney's fees using an hourly rate 50 percent higher than plaintiff counsel's customary rate.

The Third Virtue:
Making Honesty the Only Policy

*"Resolve to be honest in all events, and, if in your own judgment,
you cannot be an honest lawyer, resolve to be honest without being
a lawyer."*

—Abraham Lincoln

THE THIRD VIRTUE MEANS APPLYING President Lincoln's
advice directly to management. Resolve to be honest with
your employees "in all events." If you are a manager who values truth and integrity but cannot be steadfastly honest with
your employees, you should resolve to be honest without
being a manager. Fortunately, however, the rewards of being
honest will reinforce your resolve to be truthful. Recognize
that when you feel tempted to avoid the truth with your
employees, that feeling is probably a sign that you really
should be candid.

A Family Affair

Mary was a key employee at a small company owned by her
brother, Morton, and sister-in-law, Jill. Over time, Mary grew
restive, believing that the company would be more successful
with some changes. But her ideas were not well received.
Tensions began to surface as Mary felt frozen out from a real
leadership role and she was not offered an ownership interest
in the company. Conversely, Jill and Morton began to resent
Mary's pointed suggestions, especially since they were still
paying off a loan used to buy the business and Mary received
a higher salary than anyone else (themselves included). Mary
started complaining to other employees about how poorly the

business was being run and how if she owned her own business, Jill and Morton's company would be no competition. Mary became less accountable for her hours and work results. Jill and Morton began to worry that Mary might be secretly making plans to compete against them and sought legal advice about whether they could stop her from launching another business by filing a lawsuit.

Business, legal, and family disasters were averted, however. Jill and Morton scheduled a meeting with Mary that had only one ground rule: be honest with each other. In the meeting, they expressed their respective hopes, feelings, expectations, and frustrations. After sharing views (and a few tears), the parties decided it would be best for everyone if Mary did not continue with the business. However, Jill and Morton agreed to give her transitional assistance and support that enabled Mary to move on successfully into another, non-competitive, business endeavor. This accomplished, they—and their children—continued to participate in each others' lives, in marked contrast to so many other failures that have broken both business and family bonds.

The Benefits of Virtuous Managing

Honesty truly is the best policy—especially when the inclination to behave otherwise is strongest. An essential element of successful relationships between employer and employees is to let the latter know where they stand with the former. A boss who avoids the truth—even with the best of intentions and rationalizations—undermines trust. By contrast, habitual honesty cements faith in the relationship even if candor occasionally creates rough patches. Discomfiting as criticism can be, there is something powerfully reassuring when employees feel confident they won't be blindsided by their supervisors or undermined through passive-aggressive behavior.

To you as a manager, this means there is no downside to putting truth at the center of your relationship with your employees. At a basic human level, you demonstrate that you value your employees' dignity by being honest with them—even when the message causes pain. Abraham Lincoln liked to tell the following riddle: if you call a tail a leg, how many legs does a dog have? Answer: four. Calling a tail a leg doesn't make it a leg. When it comes to giving your employees candid feedback, resist the temptation to call a tail a leg.

Tools and Techniques

The circumstances that tempt managers to lie are predictable. Here are three ways to develop responses that will help you avoid rationalizing and practice being honest.

✔ Tip 1: Ask yourself, how would I want my boss to break this news to me?

If you know that you would prefer to hear the truth, walk that talk with your employees. Even when the news is bad and the reaction is likely to be less than pleasant, avoid rationalizing that employees are less able to deal with the truth than you are. The outcome will be worse if you're dishonest, no matter how well intentioned that dishonesty is. If you value being treated with candor in the workplace, practice this same virtue with your employees.

✓ Tip 2: Prepare to
be honest.

One of the strongest reasons for rationalizing away truth is that you fear where honesty may lead. To ensure that telling the truth won't backfire, ask yourself the following questions: If I am candid with my employees, what is their probable reaction? What questions, issues, and problems will they likely raise? What can I read or consider in advance to address their points? By thinking ahead, you leach the anxiety out of the anticipated encounter and create a solid foundation for telling the truth.

✓ Tip 3: Dismiss
and redirect.

Managers often succumb to the Third Sin when an employee tries to force them to respond at an inconvenient or difficult time. They will extricate themselves by telling a seemingly uncontroversial white lie or evasion, such as "it's really no big deal" or "don't worry about it." However, a much more constructive approach is "dismiss and redirect."

A Truthful Dock Supervisor Postpones a Discussion

An outspoken dockworker approached his harried supervisor with a demand to know why his hours were cut. The supervisor, anxious to get perishable goods unloaded, was tempted to put off the employee with a false statement. Instead, he said, "Sam, the issue you raise is serious and deserves serious discussion. However, right now we have to get these vegetables unloaded before they spoil. Tomorrow afternoon at 3:30, when your next shift begins, I will meet with you to discuss why your hours have been cut." Despite the refusal to have

Legal Nugget

Use the Attorney-Client Privilege

As several stories in this chapter show, the fear of legal liability often makes managers avoid honesty. They're afraid to say what they think is the truth. In such circumstances, it often makes sense to consult with legal counsel before you communicate with the employee. An attorney counseling session can serve as a useful way to speak your mind freely without fearing the consequences of loose lips. Not only will your attorney be able to assess the legal risk and help minimize it, but you can also speak candidly: What you say is protected by the attorney-client privilege from being discovered and used against your employer in a legal proceeding. By contrast, what you say to other managers or HR can be learned and used by a plaintiff's attorney.

Of course, this does not mean that every sensitive workplace encounter must be preceded by an attorney-client counseling session. This step applies best when management or HR learn of information presenting unusually high legal risks and need to talk openly about it before deciding what to do. If you do take this step, however, to protect your company fully you must take care thereafter to keep confidential what is said in the attorney-client session.

the discussion immediately, the supervisor communicated that the issue was important to him, too.

Just remember that to use the dismiss-and-redirect tool effectively, you must provide a *specific time* to discuss the issue. Otherwise, employees will feel put off and fear that you do not take their concerns seriously.

Chapter Three Highlights

The Third Sin: Rationalizing Away Truth

☞ Even in managers of integrity, the instinct to avoid difficult circumstances produces a desire to sidestep the truth.

☞ The manager rationalizes the urge to lean back on skis by using seemingly sound, logical reasons for doing something the gut says is not right.

☞ The result is increased risk of employee brainlock and of undermining management's credibility should it ever have to justify its decisions or actions.

☞ "Rationalize" can be seen as a two-word contraction meaning "rational lies." Examples:

- You say, "We're laying you off" when in fact you're terminating because of poor performance.
- You say, "We're terminating you because you are an 'at-will' employee" although you really don't want to be honest about the true reason.
- You give acceptable ratings for unacceptable performance to "avoid trouble."
- You add false additional justifications for an employment decision to "help support it."

☞ Managers need to realize that some employees may resort to secretly recording conversations to force their managers to admit the truth or catch them in lies.

The Third Virtue: Making Honesty the Only Policy

☛ The times when you are most tempted to avoid honesty are usually the times when honesty is most needed.

☛ No matter what your message, if you convey it with scrupulous honesty, you demonstrate respect for the dignity of your employee.

☛ Three tools or techniques can help you avoid rationalizing:

- Ask yourself, how would I want the news broken to me?
- Prepare yourself to be honest. When your candor may produce questions or concerns from your employees, anticipate, plan, and prepare for this.
- Dismiss and redirect. Instead of avoiding the truth when employees confront you at an inopportune time, tell them that what they say is important but can't be discussed at the moment. Then immediately set a specific time when you will discuss it.

☛ When tempted to avoid the truth because of legal risk, you may be able to use the attorney-client privilege to advantage by speaking openly and candidly to legal counsel, who can then help minimize risks and determine the best way to deal with the employee.

CHAPTER 4

The Fourth Sin:
Misguided Benevolence

"Hell is paved with good intentions, not bad ones."

—George Bernard Shaw

THE SIN OF MISGUIDED BENEVOLENCE OCCURS when good people make bad things happen. Negative results arise from praiseworthy motives. Management's compassion toward and understanding about employee pain or misfortune makes it forget its workplace role. Sympathy rises. Expectations, responsibility, and accountability fall. The results are in no one's best interest—not that of the company, management, coworkers, nor even the suffering employees themselves.

Kindness Begets an ADA Claim

A printing salesman, Martin, contracted cancer and underwent chemotherapy. His condition soon degenerated to the point where he could no longer drive, lift his sample cases, or focus for very long. Nevertheless, Martin asked to continue working. Katherine, the sales manager, felt great compassion and said yes.

Despite Katherine's best intentions and his colleagues' sympathetic support, Martin effectively ceased to function. On days when he felt able to come to work, Katherine dispatched other employees to pick him up, help him with any sales calls he could make, and take him home. Most of the time, Martin lay on an office couch and made occasional telephone calls. Despite this, over the next eight months Martin's compensation actually *increased*. He received his salary and all commissions on his assigned accounts even though he had little to do with the sales. Moreover, with Katherine's help, he received long-term disability payments from the company.

Eventually, the problems appeared on executive management's radar screen. In addition to noting the amount of money Martin was costing, the executives heard employees complain about spending time on his accounts without extra compensation. The company even lost a couple of his important accounts because the customers felt neglected. Executive management instructed Katherine to discharge Martin.

As Katherine later explained, she felt so compelled to shelter Martin that she never communicated about the problems and even chose not to mention them in Martin's termination interview. Instead, she selected a "neutral" word that would not hurt his feelings—"disability"—and even wrote that word on the employee exit form next to "Reason for Termination." She then provided Martin with a generous severance package. But she didn't ask for a release of claims in return.

Shortly after cashing his last severance check, Martin filed a claim under the Americans with Disabilities Act. Courtesy of the U.S. legal system, Martin subsequently received a second, more lucrative, severance package, this time in exchange for a release of claims.

All of us experience major life challenges. When employees suffer severe personal trouble with health, family, or financial matters, we naturally tend to empathize. In the proper context, such empathy is an important managerial strength. However, misguided decisions can result when workplace expectations fall and you relax, or even abandon, conduct and performance standards. Not only will you and your workplace pay a price in terms of productivity and morale, but there is seldom a happy outcome for the employee. Instead, the employee often becomes embittered and ends up suing or engaging in other harmful acts. When you abandon expectations of an employee, everyone loses.

Anger and Misguided Benevolence

A strong sign of misguided benevolence is the hostility the objects of it ultimately feel against their benefactors. In the game of golf, a chance to retake a shot without penalty is called a "mulligan." In the workplace, mulligans can lead to problems and to court. It works something like this: The problem employee messes up. Generous or sympathetic management gives the person a mulligan—a chance to try again. The employee messes up another time and again gets a mulligan. The pattern goes on until management realizes the cost is too high. Management finally declares that the employee will have to accept a penalty and move on—and feels shocked at the storm of anger that erupts.

When Providing Severance, Get a Release

The story of Katherine and Martin illustrates another point: the importance of getting a release when giving terminated employees severance benefits. Even with all of the egregious management mistakes in that case, the matter would never have surfaced in the legal system if management had required Martin to sign a release as a condition of receiving severance payments.

Employment counsel can help you craft a severance document that will stand up in your jurisdiction. Explain to the terminated employee that this is his opportunity to obtain a severance pack- age—usually payments over time or in a lump sum, and possibly with employer–paid COBRA health insurance premiums for a peri- od of time. However, be up front about the trade-off: you are doing something you don't have to (giving transitional assistance) in exchange for his doing something he doesn't have to (waiving his right to sue for any workplace claims). The concept is that the two sides part on an amicable basis.

If the employee refuses the severance because he won't sign a release, don't fret that you have inadvertently created a claim. You haven't. He would have sued anyway. This way, however, you have received an early warning to get your ducks in a row as described in the next chapter, and you have saved the money you would have otherwise spent on the severance package.

In the case of Katherine, she was outraged when Martin rewarded her endless kindness with a lawsuit. She figured that either he had been setting her up or had become so desperate for money that he lost all integrity. "I bent or broke every rule in the book for him!" she exclaimed. She couldn't fathom that he felt genuinely angry toward her and had contracted brainlock.

Managers like Katherine who have difficulty understanding such employee anger can sometimes comprehend the problem with the help of a child-rearing analogy. Imagine that you raised your children the way Katherine managed Martin. Let's say you "bent or broke every rule in the book" for your kids and rewarded every mess-up with a mulligan. You did this whether they wouldn't finish their peas, refused to do their homework, skipped class, wrecked the family car, had an out-of-wedlock teen pregnancy, or got caught in a drug bust. First, what kind of adult would emerge from such parental "benevolence"? Certainly not one an employer would be happy to hire. Second, what would the grown-up child ultimately think of you? (For a 2,600-year-old piece of wisdom on this subject, read Aesop's fable called "The Thief and His Mother.")

Misguided Benevolence: Causes a Career Stumble
The Sin of Misguided Benevolence gets committed not only when employees have serious health problems. It occurs whenever and wherever management decides to look the other way, at least in part out of sympathy.

Susan was the controller for a small but rapidly growing equipment rental company. She worked hard and, for the most part, effectively. As a single mom in her forties providing sole support for high-school-age children, she depended on the job financially. However, she existed uneasily with computers and resisted learning sophisticated financial-tracking systems despite admonitions from the general manager. But the GM did not press the point. He understood the burden that learning a major new system would create for Susan, given her home and work-life challenges.

The company was eventually acquired by a multistate outfit with sophisticated computer systems. The new entity desired to eliminate waste. Due to her lack of computer acumen, Susan got downsized. After extended unemployment, she accepted a job at half her former salary. Caught up in her day-to-day juggling act as full-time employee and single mom, she had not comprehended the importance of developing new skills—and her boss's compassionate willingness to set aside accountability did her no favors. She felt embittered and financially embattled. She contemplated legal action based on age and gender but could only afford an attorney on a contingency-fee basis. No attorney would take her case on such a basis, given her demonstrable inability to use the company's computer systems.

Stories from both ancient and contemporary parenting illustrate the point that when the senior, responsible person fails to maintain reasonable standards for a subordinate's conduct, bad things happen. In the workplace, when employment relationships end up in litigation, the following pattern is often visible in retrospect: The employee engaged in misbehavior, performed unacceptably, or had poor attendance. Management ignored, tolerated, or acquiesced to it. The consequences of the employee's actions increased and the price of management's failure to intervene continued to grow. Eventually, action had to be taken. The employee refused to accept responsibility for the problem, felt like a victim, and turned to the legal system for redress of grievances. Management was then amazed when "Mr. Mulligan" alleged discrimination, retaliation, or harassment.

The Importance of Feeling Needed in the Workplace

Well before the problem reaches the critical point, the seeds of brainlock are already being sown. Why? One reason is because work is one of the most important expressions of our lives. It gives us a sense that we've made a contribution during our short time on this planet. However, if work is disconnected from meaning, it can create malaise and a sense of purposelessness. Thus, when a benevolent boss reacts sympathetically to employees' personal, family, or health problems by suspending expectations, management unwittingly conveys a pernicious message to the already-suffering employees: "You don't count. What you do doesn't matter." This is the last message such employees need. In the storm-tossed seas of their personal lives, a benevolent manager denies them one anchor that might help: the sense that what they do at work is important, that others count on them, and that management expects and needs their positive contributions to continue.

The Fourth Virtue:
E-R-A—Expectations, Responsibility, and Accountability

"If we treat people as they can and ought to be, we help them become what they can and ought to be."

—Johann Wolfgang von Goethe

THE FOURTH VIRTUE DOES NOT MEAN eliminating empathy or compassion. Rather, it means never losing sight of workplace E-R-A—Expectations, Responsibility, and Accountability. It means understanding the importance of E-R-A not only in helping the company succeed but also in providing a sense of purpose to employees, including those suffering misfortune outside the workplace. For some employees, you may need to make extra efforts to help them. However, the focus must still remain on their meeting expectations, remaining responsible for their actions, and being accountable for results.

FDR and Harry Hopkins

As related by Doris Kearns Goodwin in *No Ordinary Time*, in the 1930s Harry Hopkins ran the Works Progress Administration for President Franklin D. Roosevelt and later was appointed secretary of commerce. When Hopkins contracted stomach cancer, surgeons had to remove three-fourths of his stomach. He literally began starving to death. At one point, doctors gave Hopkins a mere four weeks to live.

Things changed dramatically on May 10, 1940, when Nazi Germany invaded Western Europe. Roosevelt desperately needed to mobilize the United States—at that time a demilitarized, isolationist country—so that it could wage world war if necessary. He turned to Hopkins for help. Still gravely ill and in constant pain, Hopkins threw himself into developing the America's production capability, industrial capacity, and raw materials. Fellow cabinet members were amazed at the change in Hopkins' demeanor and energy. FDR leaned more and more on Hopkins for advice and support. The relationship grew to the point that the president had Hopkins move into the White House, where he became Roosevelt's No. 1 war advisor and played a critical role in creating a national production machine that stunned the world with its productivity. Hopkins remained active for more than five years after his doctors' four-weeks-to-live prognosis—outliving Roosevelt and witnessing the Allied victory. He helped arrange the Potsdam Conference in the summer of 1945 for FDR's successor, Harry S Truman. Returning to the United States, his work done, Hopkins passed away a few months later.

The Benefits of Virtuous Managing

The White House at war constitutes a highly unusual workplace. But the Hopkins-FDR story underscores the value of helping all employees, including those with major health problems, to stay connected with their work and imbued with a sense of purpose. When employees suffer from major health, family, or personal problems, it is easy for work to become neglected. As their job takes a back seat to their personal issues, a loss of connection and self-confidence ensues. The downward spiral accelerates. However, when managers practice the Fourth Virtue by combining empathy with expectations, the opportunity exists for a win-win outcome.

Tools and Techniques

Working from the principle that benevolence without expectations is misguided, consider these four steps for avoiding the Sin and practicing the Virtue.

✓ **Tip 1:** Understand the role of long-term expectations in promoting healing.

When your employees suffer inordinately, whether from a health problem, family tragedy, divorce, substance abuse, or child issues, you can certainly be sympathetic and take supportive actions. However, the best thing you can do is remain focused on long-term expectations so that employees understand that their work continues to have meaning and importance. If employees' problems render them unable to work without assistance, or continue in their present positions, or even continue in the workforce, this focus on long-term expectations will help to allow transfer or separation without brainlock. More important, the long-term perspective will create the best possible conditions for the employee to get better, at work and otherwise.

A Tough Coach Stays Tough

As related in Ken Blanchard and Don Shula's book *Everyone's a Coach*, Miami Dolphins special-teams coach Mike Westhoff contracted bone cancer and underwent chemotherapy. When Westhoff wanted to continue doing his job, Coach Shula gave him the opportunity, accommodating Westhoff's physical limitations without relaxing expectations. Westhoff showed up at training camp "with crutches, a giant brace, and no hair." He frequently vomited at work. One day at practice, Westhoff and Shula got into an argument over the relative merits of a kicker. The gaunt Westhoff and barrel-chested Shula went at it, toe to toe, as Shula "made sure I'd done my homework," Westhoff reported. At home that night, for the first time in a long while, Westhoff ate and digested a full meal. Eventually he fully recovered and continued a successful coaching career, winning recognition for his inspiring personal example. Westhoff in turn credited Shula, whom he described as "very demanding, even when I was sick with cancer. . . Don Shula never looked at me as if I were handicapped. He sees what you can be, not what you are."

✔ **Tip 2:** Return employees to work
          to get them well.

In recent years, there has been a shift in thinking regarding employees who miss work due to on-the-job injuries and who are covered by workers' compensation. Conventional wisdom once held that injured workers should stay home to heal, then return. However, later studies revealed an alarming finding: the longer injured workers remained at home, the more likely they were to become depressed, lose confidence in their ability to function, and *never* return to work. Injuries that could have been overcome turned into cases of permanent, total disability. As a result, most employers now have modified-duty programs in which they proactively look for ways to keep injured employees at work by assigning tasks that are consistent with their medical restrictions. The employees continue working while they mend. When they have recovered, the employers return them to their former positions.

"Reasonable Accommodation" and Performance Standards

The Americans with Disabilities Act entitles employees with mental or physical impairments that substantially limit them in major life activities to "reasonable accommodation." Some state laws define "disability" more liberally than the ADA. Thus, you may have a legal duty to help employees with serious health problems. This may include adjusting working or environmental conditions, changing schedules, eliminating nonessential duties, or providing job aids and other forms of assistance. Employees may also be entitled to a leave of absence as a disability accommodation, or may otherwise be entitled to a leave of absence under the Family Medical Leave Act or state law. Even if employees cannot be reasonably accommodated, you may have an obligation to transfer them to available jobs that they can perform, with or without a reasonable accommodation.

But does reasonable accommodation include lowering performance standards? If these standards are legitimate, job-related, and consistently applied, the answer is no. So avoid lowering performance standards to levels that would otherwise be unacceptable. Your focus should be on helping employees achieve workplace expectations notwithstanding their impairments or disabilities—for their sake as well as yours. With employment counsel's help, you can and should maintain this line.

The lessons of the Fourth Virtue apply here. Keeping employees connected to their employer helps them recover by giving physical rehabilitation a sense of purpose beyond simply mending the body. In this respect, the Fourth Virtue also provides a cautionary insight to employers. To give employees that sense of purpose, a modified-duty program must itself have meaning, and E-R-A (Expectations, Responsibility, and Accountability) must be maintained. If the modified-duty assignments appear unimportant or demeaning, they may backfire and reinforce the injured workers' sense of hopelessness. (This is a good reason not to call such assignments "light" duty.)

✓ **Tip 3:** Focus on your E-R-A.

One of the principal measures of a baseball pitcher's effectiveness is the ERA, or Earned Run Average. The same measure can be applied to the manager who strives to throw the "right pitches" to employees at the right times and under the right conditions. In management baseball, E-R-A stands for, as mentioned before, Expectations, Responsibility, and Accountability. A manager with all-star E-R-A maintains substantial expectations of employees. She expects them to be responsible for their actions and accountable for results. Throughout the season, she simultaneously tracks her own and her employees' E-R-As by asking questions such as: What are my expectations of my employees? Have I communicated the expectations effectively? Are they meeting them? When it comes to getting their jobs done right and on time, who is primarily responsible—the employees or me? Do I delegate responsibility, dump it, or hoard it? Are my employees accountable—to themselves, to me, and to each other?

A CEO Changes His Plan with a Willful Employee

The CEO of a publishing company wanted to fire his long-time office manager. No stranger to serious challenges of his own, the CEO had in the past sympathized with the office manager's personal problems and given her a number of mulligans. However, the company's markets and profit margins had shrunk dramatically. New technologies and competition required more sophisticated skills as well as a special emphasis on customer relations. Meanwhile, the office manager clung to yesterday's practices and made it clear that if her interpersonal style seemed less than warm and fuzzy, her attitude was, "Well, too bad."

The CEO was concerned about firing the office manager because she was a woman in her mid-fifties. He therefore sought advice from employment counsel. Counsel and the CEO first examined the CEO's E-R-A. Perceiving that he had failed to communicate with the office manager about expectations, responsibilities, and accountabilities, the CEO changed his plan. He met with the office manager to describe the gaps in her performance and his expectations in light of industry and market challenges. He offered to make coaching and training available. However, he emphasized that the responsibility to close the gaps rested with her, that her progress would be measured, that she would be held accountable for results—and that substantial improvement had to occur for her employment to continue. After the meeting, he shared a summary of his points with her in a memo that he then used to track results.

Focusing on E-R-A proved highly successful. Several months later, the CEO reported that to his own surprise, she had become one of his best employees. He no longer needed legal advice on terminating an employee in legally protected classes.

✔ **Tip 4:** Focus on effect,
                not cause.

Many managers run afoul of employment laws by focusing on the traits, characteristics, or personal circumstances that led an employee to fall below expectations. The deeper the managers probe into the employee's drinking problem, bankruptcy, domestic issues, or health troubles, the further they travel down the slippery slope to the legal system. A much safer approach is to focus instead on effect, not cause. Ask yourself, "What is it about the employee's performance, conduct, or attendance that creates problems?" Do not ask, "What is going on in this worker's personal life that may be causing or contributing to these problems?"

You should not be insensitive to your employees' personal lives. Nevertheless, the greater your focus on workplace performance, the greater the likelihood that your decisions will be sound from a management perspective and won't get second-guessed in court.

Chapter Four Highlights

The Fourth Sin: Misguided Benevolence

☛ It is a mistake to allow sympathy for employees' personal problems to suspend workplace expectations and accountability.

☛ This Sin hurts not only the company, the manager, and coworkers, but it also hurts the afflicted employees by disconnecting them from a sense of meaning or purpose in the workplace.

☛ Despite having been given many mulligans, or extra chances, such employees often come to hate their benefactors and seek revenge through the legal system.

☛ Parenting provides a useful analogy. Children raised without standards, expectations, or accountability grow into adults whom no one would want to employ and who hate their parents.

☛ Don't overlook the importance of getting a release in exchange for severance benefits—even in situations where providing such benefits is beneficently motivated.

The Fourth Virtue: E-R-A, or Expectations, Responsibility, and Accountability

☛ Maintaining real and substantial performance expectations of all employees is healthiest for everyone.

☛ Expectations should not block out a manager's compassion for a suffering employee; rather, expectations provide the context in which such compassion should be expressed.

☛ An employee's health problem may trigger legal duties, such as making an accommodation or providing a leave of absence; however, this does not mean reducing performance expectations.

☛ Instead of having employees on workers' compensation stay away from work to heal completely and then return, it is more effective to help them heal back *at* work. For modified-duty assignments, managers must still maintain E-R-A and provide work with a sense of purpose or meaning.

☛ Focus on your and your employees' E-R-A. Assess the following:
- What are your expectations of your employees? How have you communicated the expectations?
- Who takes primary responsibility for your employees' successful job performance: you, them, someone else, or no one?
- To whom are they accountable for their performances: you, them, someone else, or no one? How are they held accountable? What gets measured?

☛ When an employee's performance falls below expectations, focus on effect, not cause.

- A "cause" focus often leads the employer into a thicket of legally regulated issues such as health, disability, and family matters.

- An "effect" focus tends to remain within the legal discretion and prerogative of employers to maintain workplace expectations.

CHAPTER 5

The Fifth Sin:
Falling into the Inconsistency Trap

"When you come to a fork in the road, take it."

—Yogi Berra

IN THEIR HASTE TO GET EVERYTHING done, managers continually and unwittingly fall into four inconsistency traps: (1) person to person, (2) person to document, (3) document to document, and (4) person over time. The consequence of managerial inconsistency tends to be employee brainlock and, if brainlock leads to legal action, a defense may be difficult for management to maintain.

Inconsistency Leads to Sexual Harassment and Retaliation Claims

Barbara, the manager of an apartment complex, worked patiently with her young leasing agent, Amy. The two got along well personally and had developed a big sister/little sister relationship. However, Amy had problems involving attendance, erroneously applied rent payments, a short fuse with coworkers and residents, and sometimes coming to work in sexually provocative attire. Barbara gave Amy many "second chances" as she coached, encouraged, cajoled, and scolded the leasing agent.

Reluctantly, Barbara began to conclude that Amy had to be let go. However, before she could act, Amy asserted that she had been sexually harassed by a maintenance worker. After mentioning to a group of employees that she had accepted a part-time job at an exotic dance club, the maintenance worker had asked, "Will you strip?" Amy interpreted his question as, "Will you strip now, in front of us?"

Barbara promptly investigated. The maintenance worker explained that he had meant, "Will you strip at the club?" and readily apologized for any misunderstanding and hurt feelings. After Amy told Barbara that she had accepted his apology, Barbara considered the matter successfully resolved.

Two weeks later, Barbara issued a written warning stating that Amy faced termination for any further performance and conduct problems—a warning like ones Barbara had given in the past but never enforced. One week later, Amy applied a rent check to the wrong apartment and then got into a shouting match with the resident who complained about it. Reluctantly deciding that enough was enough, Barbara fired Amy.

Amy promptly brought claims of sexual harassment and retaliation. Her lawyer acknowledged that the harassment claim was weak but hammered on the retaliation claim. In addition to the close timing of the discharge to Amy's internal complaint, he cited a cornucopia of inconsistencies: (a) Barbara's failure to follow the disciplinary procedure in the employee handbook; (b) inconsistencies within the handbook itself on attendance and performance expectations; (c) inconsistencies between the reasons cited for discharge and documents in Amy's personnel file, including a recent "satisfactory" performance evaluation; and (d) prior written warnings of discharge that Barbara had never followed up on. As a result of these inconsistencies, a demonstrably poor employee received a substantial settlement to release her claims.

The Four Basic Inconsistency Traps

Managers are typically unaware of their inconsistencies until the problems are thrust under their noses by a brainlocked employee or, worse, the employee's attorney. Barbara did not consciously choose to be inconsistent. She simply never stopped to think about it and just reacted to the situation before her. Only later did the response prove problematic.

Here are four basic inconsistency traps that lead to brainlock and litigation.

Trap 1: Person-to-person inconsistency.
This most common trap arises when one employee gets paid less, disciplined more, passed over for a promotion, or otherwise treated less favorably than someone else who performs similarly. The result is often brainlock that may lead to a lawsuit. But even with no legal action, this inconsistency—or the perception that it exists—greatly undermines morale, trust, and teamwork.

Trap 2: Person-to-document inconsistency.
This trouble arises when management treats employees in a way that is inconsistent with the company's official docu-

ments, such as procedural manuals, employee handbooks, policy memoranda, e-mail messages, or human resources documents. For example, a manager terminates an employee for erratic attendance. Yet in a performance evaluation two months earlier—based on a desire to avoid conflict (the First Sin) and on rationalization ("I didn't want to discourage her," the Third Sin)—the supervisor had checked off "acceptable" in the very category for which he has now fired her. Another example: In her haste, a manager does not bother to consult company policies and procedures to see whether she's complying with what these documents say. She then contradicts written company policy. The contradiction not only generates anger but impeaches her credibility.

Trap 3: Document-to-document inconsistency.

Sometimes a company's documents contradict each other. The larger, the more diversified, and the more geographically dispersed a company is, the greater the likelihood of inconsistent documents. But the problem can arise anywhere. For example, the head of a department distributes a memo regarding scheduling vacations. However, because she fails to check the policies-and-procedures manual, she does not realize that her memo contradicts the official rules. Another example: a CFO responds to a question regarding incentive compensation, not knowing that the CEO had just addressed the same topic with another employee in a way that did not square with the CFO's views. A third example: a supervisor issues a written reprimand to an employee but, having not reviewed any documents beforehand, doesn't realize he is criticizing the employee for failure to perform a function that was never in the written job description.

Trap 4: Person-over-time inconsistency.

This typically arises in two circumstances. First, a "beginning skier" supervisor is succeeded by one who resolutely keeps her weight forward on skis. For most of the work crew, the change is a breath of fresh air. For a few, however, it seems oppressive because what was once acceptable no longer is.

Second, a supervisor has been leaning back on skis for a long time. Eventually, he can take it no longer and confronts a problem employee, letting loose his pent-up frustrations. He is like a skier who, after leaning back on his skis for a long time, throws his weight forward so forcefully that he winds up plunging face first into the snow. The employee now being lambasted feels victimized since his (under) performance has been consistent but the supervisor's response has not.

There is perhaps no faster path to the legal system than through management inconsistency. An employee's attorney will pounce on it, especially when it can be linked to a claim of discriminatory treatment. The typical path goes like this. You take some form of "adverse employment action," such as discharge; demotion; or denial of a job, promotion, or wage increase. The disgruntled employee then asserts that your motivation is race, gender, age, disability, religion, national origin, or other protected job classification, or that you are retaliating for a legally protected activity. An attorney will use inconsistencies to undermine your credibility and the legitimacy of the reasons you offer for the action.

What constitutes "protected activity" varies from state to state and jurisdiction to jurisdiction. Examples of such activity are

Legal Nugget

Conduct a Litigation Post-Mortem

If a claim has been brought against your company and has been resolved (whether by settlement or adjudication), resist the temptation to put the painful experience out of mind. Instead, conduct a post-mortem. With your attorney's help, analyze how and why the claim came to exist and what helped or hurt the company. Ask questions such as: Did we, in fact, do something wrong? Do our policies and practices comply with applicable federal and state laws? Are there any policies or practices that create an unnecessary or avoidable risk of liability? Were our policies consistently followed? Were the problems or issues with the employee promptly and properly documented? Were opportunities to head off the claim missed? If there were unemployment compensation proceedings, did we get information about what the employee was claiming before his attorney was involved? Did we exacerbate the problem by making contradictory or unsupportable statements that were used against us? What was done right? What helped defend the claim or prevent it from becoming worse?

The answers to these questions provide valuable insights that will help prevent future claims. More important, if management acts quickly on the knowledge gained, the still-fresh pain of recently concluded litigation will provide momentum for constructive change.

an employee's complaints about alleged harassment, discrimination, or safety; raising health issues; or threatening legal action based on alleged wrongful employer acts.

Inconsistencies that lead to discrimination claims may also include treating an employee not in the plaintiff's protected class more favorably under similar circumstances, or taking action long after an employee's deficient conduct first showed itself—such as soon after the employee engaged in some form of protected activity. Plaintiff's counsel will seize on these inconsistencies as proof that you harbor an ulterior motive forbidden by law—and that you do not manage by your own rules.

The Fifth Virtue:
Ducks in a Row

"Chaos was the law of nature; order was the dream of man."

—Henry Adams

THE FIFTH VIRTUE MEANS ESTABLISHING order out of what might otherwise be chaos. It means thinking "ducks in a row" (and getting them there) *before* taking action. Such advance thinking helps management stay out of the inconsistency trap and dramatically reduces the odds of creating brainlock or of receiving an unwelcome invitation to the legal system.

Ducks in a Row Avoids a Lawsuit

Two employees at adjacent workstations in a telemarketing department got into a shouting match about which of them talked too loudly on the telephone. One man threatened to beat up the other. Following an investigation, management reprimanded one of the employees (who was white) and fired the other (who was African-American). The latter filed a claim with the Equal Employment Opportunity Commission claiming inconsistency in treatment and citing the overall paucity of black employees as evidence of race discrimination.

During the agency investigation, the employer showed that before deciding what discipline to impose, management had addressed the question of inconsistency. After reviewing personnel files, company policy documents, and past situations, executives decided there would be no inconsistency because only the African-American threatened violence. The employer produced the employee handbook policy—which expressly forbade threats of violence and subjected a violator to termination on the first offense—and presented the black employee's signed acknowledgment that he had received the handbook. The employer also showed that it had applied this policy consistently in the past. Without evidence of inconsistency or of any policies or practices that worked to exclude blacks, the mere paucity of African-Americans was insufficient to sustain a claim. As a result, the EEOC found for the employer, and the employee dropped the claim rather than file a lawsuit.

Today's litigious times make practicing the Fifth Virtue more important than ever. When every management inconsistency is another arrow in plaintiff counsel's quiver, getting ducks in a row first makes compelling sense. It is surprisingly easy to avoid the inconsistency trap by developing the right mindset. Unlike Pavlov's famous dogs, which salivated automatically upon hearing a bell even when there was no food waiting for them, you as a manager have the ability to insert thought between stimulus and response. Otherwise, if you react to stimuli as did Pavlov's hungry dogs, you will experience similar disappointments.

Tools and Techniques

Here are several tips for avoiding inconsistency and getting your ducks in a row before you make and execute a workplace decision.

✔ **Tip 1:** Take both the subjective and
　　　　objective test of inconsistency.

The test for determining consistency should be both *subjective* and *objective*. You first need to ask whether *you* think there *is* an inconsistency (the subjective test). On innumerable occasions, if management had asked itself this simple question before acting, disaster would have been averted. In hiring, promotion, transfer, pay, or disciplinary decisions, it takes less than an ounce of preventive effort to ask whether similar circumstances have arisen before and, if so, how they were handled.

If you pass the subjective test, you then need to ask whether you can demonstrate that no inconsistency exists (the objective test). In sensitive situations where someone's job may be at stake, it is important to be able to demonstrate that your decisions are consistent. You need proof to fend off a threatened claim. Moreover, by being able to show why something that initially appears inconsistent is not, you will go a long way toward avoiding brainlock and producing acceptance of your decision.

A Company Passes the Subjective Test But Fails the Objective One

While driving a construction vehicle across a temporary construction road, a Mexican-American employee looked out the driver's-side window while carrying on a conversation with a coworker on the ground. As a result, the driver did not see a large rock in the center of the otherwise smooth road and drove directly over it, blowing out a tire. Repairing the damage to the vehicle cost several thousand dollars.

The site manager fired the driver for negligent operation of equipment. But first the manager asked himself whether there might be an inconsistency in doing so, since Anglo employees had blown tires and not been fired. The manager decided there was no inconsistency because (a) the other employees operated different types of vehicles under conditions that were actually more hazardous; and (b) the other situations did not involve carelessness, such as looking away and talking while driving.

Unfortunately for his company, the manager failed to ask the second question: Can I *show* that there is no inconsistency? When the ex-employee asserted a discrimination claim several months later, no documentation or photographs existed. The haul road no longer existed, and both the tire and the equipment in question—which had been leased—were gone. Employees who could have been witnesses had moved on. No documentation existed regarding the Anglo employees either. The employer was left with the manager's recollection of the events, which, not surprisingly, differed from the terminated employee's in every material respect. Instead of a well-documented, well-supported presentation of the differences between white employees' flat tires and the Mexican-American's, management had a major legal battle on its hands, one it paid a substantial amount to settle.

✓ **Tip 2:** In getting your ducks in a row, ask the following key questions.
Are there any legal potholes that I need to be aware of? Although it's virtually impossible to find a list of all state

and federal laws and regulations that an employment decision might trigger, managers continually get into trouble by failing even to pose this question when they make status-changing decisions, such as to hire, promote, demote, or fire. At a minimum, you as a manager (with the assistance of HR or employment counsel) should ask yourself whether employees who will be affected fall into legally protected classes and, if so, whether employees who perform similarly but are not in any of the same protected classes have been treated differently. Has the employee recently engaged in conduct that might be deemed protected activity?

Have we created brainlock, or are we in danger of doing so? This question is especially pertinent if you are contemplating inflicting "injury" on an employee or job applicant and wish to avoid the unintentional insult. Ask yourself: Has the employee been given an opportunity to express a point of view? Was the viewpoint considered? Have we been honest with the employee? Did we explain the reasons for our decision? Does the manner in which we plan to execute our decision respect the dignity of the employee? If I were in the employee's shoes, how would I want the news broken?

Am I gathering information or actually making a decision? Managers create a great deal of trouble for themselves when they confuse their investigator or information-gatherer role with their decision-maker role. Whenever you must make a decision that requires collecting evidence (and this covers most decisions), you should complete your research *first*. When you blur the sequence between information gathering and deciding, you often create a sense of unfairness and risk employee brainlock and legal claims. This means you should complete harassment investigations before you tell anyone of the consequences. You should gather information about performance or conduct failure, including questioning the employee, before you decide on the discipline. When you jump the gun by announcing your intentions without completing the procedural steps, your impulsiveness calls into question the credibility of the entire process. Even sound decisions appear unsound. Observations of numerous cases of brainlock and resulting litigation show that one cannot emphasize enough the importance of respecting the process of decision making and not just the result. Indeed, *how* you make your decision is often more important than *what* you decide.

What documents should I read? You can avoid a great many claims as well as negative confrontations by following a simple directive: read your documents! When contemplating decisions that may affect an employee's status, ask: are there any potentially relevant documents I should read first? Such documents may include policies and procedures contained in the employee handbook or the personnel or operations manual; the employee's personnel file; documents on how other, similar cases were handled; memoranda issued by management; written statements of the company's mission, values, or goals; e-mail communications; and correspondence. If the decision will be significant, it is always best when you read the relevant documents before the employee does—or before the employee's lawyer does.

✔ **Tip 3:** Pave the way to change by communicating "That was then, this is now."

Companies reorganize. They adopt initiatives. They face new challenges in the marketplace, in industry, or in technology that require them to place new demands and requirements on their workforces. But even when change occurs on a smaller scale, employees still feel it. Supervisors may attend a training program, read a book, or engage in some other self-improvement exercise and decide to change the way they oversee their employees. Whether on a small scale or large one, and whether for good or for ill, these changes create the fourth type of inconsistency: time. Employees find themselves being treated differently even though their performance has not changed.

However, such inconsistency will not necessarily land you in trouble as long as you communicate the change with a simple but clear message, borrowing from the title of an S.E. Hinton book: *That Was Then, This Is Now*. Before imposing new rules, conditions, or expectations, and before holding employees accountable for them, you need to mark the passage from "then" to "now." Doing so greatly improves the odds of implementing change successfully—without causing brainlock in the process.

✔ **Tip 4:** Make skillful use of the concept of amnesty.

Granting employees amnesty means giving them a clean slate despite past infractions. You will determine future advancement or discipline from the point at which you've given amnesty, and not before. The amnesty message may make sense if you decide to change your supervisory habits after recognizing that you are guilty of Sins of Mismanagement. Let's say you have been leaning back on your skis; failing to be direct, immediate, and specific; rationalizing instead of being scrupulously honest; and engaging in misguided benevolence or inconsistency. The best approach may be to combine a that-was-then, this-is-now message with amnesty for past problems in performance or conduct that you failed to deal with properly.

If you do apply the amnesty tool, be careful. It can become overused and counterproductive. Paradoxically, it allows you to avoid confronting a difficult employee problem even as you profess to do just that. Perhaps you announce, "That was then, this is now. We can no longer tolerate tardiness, but we will begin this new phase by giving you amnesty for past violations." Then six months go by without holding employees accountable for recent infractions. You decide to make another fresh start, reissuing amnesty and sending a new "that was then, this is now" message. The pattern repeats itself until you sound like the boy who cried wolf.

Most cases will not require amnesty. "That was then, this is now" will be sufficient to point out to employees that your study of the past and forecast of the future indicates that it's time for change. The focus is not on forgiveness for past misdeeds but on the path to a successful future. Nevertheless, amnesty may be appropriate when all of the following conditions exist:

■ You as a manager have repeatedly committed serious inconsistencies or other sins in your treatment of employees.

- You are *committed* to changing your relationship with employees and skiing the run, as in the example to follow about a warehouse manager who set a "three strikes you're out" policy.
- Employees receiving amnesty have not committed a recent infraction so serious that they legitimately deserve to be terminated or strongly disciplined.

Amnesty in Action

A large food distributor had a major attendance problem at one of its warehouses, which caused delays, mistakes, and inefficiencies in loading and unloading trucks. Due to increased industry competition and shrinking profit margins, the company could no longer tolerate the problem. The warehouse manager called a meeting to announce a new policy with two provisions: (a) amnesty, in that past attendance infractions were wiped clean; and (b) "three strikes you're out," meaning that three future attendance infractions would result in immediate discharge. He distributed this policy to all employees and had them sign a written acknowledgment that they had received and understood it. He also posted the policy.

The first (and only) person to violate the three-strikes-you're-out provision happened to be the only African-American employee. His historical attendance record was much better than that of several white employees. After his firing, he asserted a race discrimination claim and retained a prominent plaintiff's attorney. In response, the employer's attorney presented opposing counsel with evidence of the "that was then, this is now" meeting, the posted notice, the employee's signed acknowledgment, and case law showing that such changes were within management's discretion and did not support an inference of racial animus. The employee's attorney then withdrew, and the employee dropped the claim.

Chapter Five Highlights

The Fifth Sin: Falling into the Inconsistency Trap

☛ Too often, managers get caught in one of four inconsistency traps:

- Person-to-person inconsistency: treating two employees differently in similar circumstances or conditions.
- Person-to-document inconsistency: treating an employee in ways that are contrary to provisions of an employee handbook, policy manual, memorandum, e-mail messages, performance evaluation, or other documents.
- Document-to-document inconsistency: following workplace documents that contradict each other.
- Person-over-time inconsistency: treating an employee differently over time for the same behavior, often when a new supervisor takes over or an existing supervisor gets fed up with an employee's pattern of behavior.

☛ Management inconsistency creates brainlock and provides the means for plaintiff's counsel to attack the company's credibility while seeking to prove that management's true motivation is race, gender, religion, national origin, age, or disability discrimination; unlawful retaliation; or other impermissible bases.

☛ When you have been sued, as soon as the case ends, conduct a post-mortem analyzing how and why the claim came to be made and what policies, practices, and procedures exposed the company to liability or aided in its defense.

The Fifth Virtue: Ducks in a Row

☞ Getting ducks in a row before you take action avoids brainlock and exposure to legal claims.

☞ It means inserting *thought* between stimulus and response.

☞ Consistency must be objective, not merely subjective; you must be able to demonstrate it.

☞ To evaluate your actions, you need to ask these questions:
  ■ Is there an inconsistency?
  ■ Can I show that there isn't?
  ■ What legal potholes do I need to be aware of?
  ■ Are we in danger of creating brainlock?
  ■ Am I wearing the information-gatherer hat or decision-maker hat?
  ■ What documents do I need to read?

☞ When employees face substantial change in workplace conditions or expectations, they need a clear message regarding the nature of the change and the path forward. This message can be called "That was then, this is now."

☞ When the change has to do with moving from lax management to weight forward on skis, it may be appropriate to give employees amnesty for past infractions and start with a clean slate.

☛ However, you shouldn't be too quick to use the amnesty tool. You must be committed to walk the new talk and the employees should not have committed any recent significant infractions.

CHAPTER 6

The Sixth Sin:
Letting Employees Speculate

"Make not your thoughts your prisons."

—William Shakespeare, *Antony and Cleopatra*

THE SIXTH SIN OF MISMANAGEMENT IS DEADLY because of the Law of Employee Speculation, which holds that if employees don't know, they will speculate. And when they speculate, their suspicions are *always* worse than reality. Thus, in virtually every instance, management is better off sharing information than withholding it. Yet numerous managers are either indifferent to sharing information or see their role as guardians of information. They unwittingly set the Law of Employee Speculation into motion, creating unnecessary risks of employment litigation and undermining their organizations' ability to get the best from their employees.

The following are three examples of the Law of Employee Speculation in action.

Employee Speculation Leads to a
Rash of Discrimination Claims

An employer investigated an internal claim that a female employee had been denied equal pay and that her department

---

Legal Nugget

Confidentiality and Settlement or Separation Agreements

In most instances, it makes sense for an employer settling a claim or providing severance benefits through a separation agreement to include a provision requiring the employee to keep the terms confidential. However, these provisions should be one-way and not bind the employer to keep information confidential if the employer deems some form of disclosure necessary or appropriate to administer its business affairs. Circumstances may call for disclosure. Moreover, if negative employee speculation takes off as in the cases described here, management may need to apply the brakes by getting the word out to employees that the company did not break the bank to settle the claim.

---

head had retaliated against her for complaining about it. The investigation confirmed every charge. The company fired the department head, "promoted" the employee to the job she was already doing, and paid her $15,000 for lost wages in exchange for a release of claims. Management felt great about this resolution. The company had not only done the right thing, but it had also avoided a lawsuit it almost certainly would have lost, with damages much greater than the settlement amount.

The settlement agreement included the customary confidentiality clause, strictly forbidding the employee from disclosing terms of the settlement. Technically speaking, she kept her end of the bargain. When coworkers pressed for details, she dutifully replied that the company had made her sign an agreement not to say anything. However, it did not help matters when, shortly after the settlement, she pulled into the employee parking lot in her new Cadillac and stepped out of her car wearing her new fur coat.

The Law of Employee Speculation took hold. Her coworkers guessed that she never would have settled for less than $300,000 and might have gotten as much as $600,000. Management picked up some clues that employees were speculating about settlement and using widely exaggerated figures. However, sticking to its self-perceived "guardian of information" role, it did nothing to correct the misperceptions. It simply repeated the injunction that such information was strictly confidential. As a result, the company ended up having many opportunities to assess the Law of Employee Speculation at work. Over the next few years, it had to defend *sixty* claims of gender discrimination.

The Union Takes a Perk to Arbitration

A major symphony orchestra faced increasing challenges with retaining subscribers and donors. In a move that greatly upset the musicians, management responded to audiences' changing tastes by increasing the amount of pops concerts and other nonclassical programming. To ease the musicians' artistic pain, management then announced a counterbalancing move—the creation of a chamber orchestra emphasizing the work of classical and baroque composers such as Mozart, Haydn, Bach, and Vivaldi.

Management was shocked when the musicians' union filed a grievance claiming that the new chamber ensemble constituted a unilateral change in the collective-bargaining agreement in violation of federal labor law. But management was even more shocked once it learned why. No one had bothered to explain the reason for the change, assuming it to be self-evident. So the musicians filled in the communication gap by reckoning that the creation of a chamber orchestra was a nefarious ploy to fire musicians. In smaller ensembles, each musician's sound is more identifiable—which is normally wonderfully pleasing to a serious musician. Here, however, orchestra members assumed management would now pick off hapless musicians by asserting that their playing was deficient.

When he learned the thinking behind the union grievance, the orchestra's executive director shook his head in amazement, exclaiming, "With our union agreement and culture, we *never* fire musicians. You would have to go after the conductor with a machete to lose your job!"

Invasion of the Robots

For tax-planning and capital-investment purposes, a manufacturing company decided to sell its land, building, and fixtures to an investment group while receiving a ninety-nine-year lease to remain on the property and continue operations. Nothing would change regarding the manufacturing operation. The company simply switched from being an owner to a lessee. For employees, the transaction was—or should have been—a nonevent. Unfortunately, however, management neglected to inform them of its plans and said nothing when the investment group sent representatives to inspect and evaluate the plant.

Although the transaction with the investment group went without a hitch, disturbing changes began to occur. Turnover increased. A quiescent union rumbled to life with a spate of grievances and, for the first time in years, demands for arbitration. Employee theft increased. Employment discrimination claims were filed.

When HR investigated the causes of these developments, it encountered the Law of Employee Speculation. A rumor had ripened into perceived truth. Employees decided that the investment group's inspectors came from a *robot maker* and that management was secretly planning to replace them with robots. The real invasion came not from mechanical contraptions duplicating the work of human beings; it came from the imaginations of employees who filled a void in workplace communication.

Most managers fail to appreciate the importance of information flow in a successful employer-employee relationship. It is true that some information should not be shared. However, managers are far more likely to err on the side of under-disclosure, as opposed to over-disclosure. Combining the adage "knowledge is power" with the beginning-skier instinct to lean back, they recognize only the downside of letting information out, not the downside of failing to share it. They don't see how the Law of Employee Speculation will fill the vacuum their silence creates. The failure to share information has led many employers to the legal system

Legal Nugget

If the Company Won't Fill in a Reason, Employees Will

Many managers avoid telling a terminated employee the reason for discharge. Their beginning-skier instinct tells them to avoid an argument, and they figure that since the employee is at-will, they do not have to have a reason. Managers who think that way should consider this observation from an intake worker for an anti-discrimination agency: "If the employer told employees why they were being fired, half of them wouldn't even have come here to file a claim." She described a recurring pattern in which an employer fires an employee without stating the reason and the employee fills in the blank by assuming the cause was age, gender, race, national origin, or other protected class status. Had management been straightforward and truthful, these claims would have been prevented.

The study of discharges in Ohio described in Chapter Two also addressed the correlation between giving information about reasons for termination and the likelihood that a claim would be filed. According to the study, employees who were not informed of management's reason for discharging them were at least *ten times* more likely to sue than those given a reason, regardless of what the reason was.

when they could have easily avoided the trip. The following story is representative.

An Equal Pay Question Converts to a Claim

Although unsure of the facts, a female employee in a retail store felt she was underpaid in relation to a male coworker and complained to her boss about the perceived disparity. He could have made several legitimate points about differences in positions as well as erroneous assumptions she was making. However, the supervisor feared litigation and refused to discuss the issue. His refusal confirmed in her mind that she was a victim of discrimination. She filed a claim. In the course of the legal proceedings, the employer eventually provided the information she had requested and prevailed. By then, however, the employer had wasted substantial time and money while witnessing the destruction of a formerly productive relationship between supervisor and employee. Eventually, the employer gave her a severance package in exchange for her agreement to leave the company and sign a release.

The Sixth Virtue:
Open Information Channels

"Information is the oxygen of the modern age."

—Ronald Reagan

ADOPTING THE SIXTH VIRTUE MEANS that creating an information-rich work environment becomes a top organizational priority. Employees feel empowered and respected when management provides information generously. Even if the news isn't good, sharing it is almost always better than withholding it. Management's focus, therefore, should be on opening the channels and letting the information flow.

An Unconventional Workforce Reorganization with No Bitter Ending

A company planned to close its facility once it completed construction on a new facility in another state. It eschewed the conventional wisdom to hold its cards close to the vest regarding sharing its plans with employees. Early on, it announced its intentions and stated it would keep employees fully abreast of developments. It began a newsletter to address the changes and impending RIFs. It set up an employee hotline for questions or concerns and established interactive communications in which the company shared information about what it knew and did not yet know. If employees raised questions for which management did not have immediate answers, it reported back when the answers were learned. The company communicated information regarding job-reduction schedules, severance benefits, retirement and health questions, and employment opportunities in the community.

The company maintained this approach during nearly eighteen months of transition, with the surprising result that profits *increased.* Instead of anger, bitterness, or brainlock, employees displayed loyalty and diligence even as they faced job loss.

The benefits of sharing information go well beyond avoiding the Law of Employee Speculation or keeping the legal system at bay. The advantages go to the heart of an effective employer-employee relationship. When you entrust employees with all possible information relevant to their employment, you do not just avoid speculation. You enable employees to achieve their potential.

The presumption should therefore be in favor of disclosing information, not withholding it. The question should be "Why not?" as opposed to "Why?" You should ask: What information do my employees need? What information would I need if I were in their shoes? What information do I need from them? Who needs to be in the loop? If I withhold this information because of its sensitivity, will the negative consequences of withholding it outweigh the potential problems of disclosing it?

Tools and Techniques

Here are tips for a few common situations when information sharing would help prevent claims and increase organizational effectiveness.

✔ **Tip 1:** When informing an employee of termination, be candid and diplomatic.

As noted earlier, management should always tell an employee why he is losing his job. However, this does not mean presenting a bill of particulars summarizing in detail all misdeeds leading to the decision. The following statements usually work: "As we have previously addressed, your sales levels have continued to fall below what we need and expect. As a result, we have unfortunately concluded that the fit is not right and it is necessary to terminate your employment." Or: "Based on our investigation, we have concluded that your conduct [summarize briefly] violates important company policy and values. As a result, we no longer have the trust and confidence necessary for your employment to continue, and we are ending it today."

If the employee argues with your reasons, listen with the techniques provided in Chapter Seven. Then conclude, "I understand that you view the matter differently than we do, but this is a decision we feel we have to make." If the employee becomes disputatious, short-circuit the volatility with a technique called "channeling." For example, you could say, "Pat, we're not here to argue with you. Obviously, you see things very differently and are angry with us. I think this means both sides will be better off if we part company and you find a better fit with another employer." In this way, management "channels" the employee's anger at being fired away from a desire to prove that the company is evil (brainlock) to the thought that the company is beneath him (moving on elsewhere). The employee hears the reason for discharge and is given a controlled opportunity to express his disagreement—as opposed to being left to speculate about the injustice of it all.

✓ **Tip 2:** Give employees the minimum information
they need to calm speculation about
terminations.

When you fire someone, how much information should you
share with other employees? A natural management tendency is to seal the information tight out of fear of legal or other
consequences. Although discretion is important, sealing
information may trigger the Law of Employee Speculation
and create more trouble than limited disclosure would.

Refusing to share information about an employee's discharge
may cause the following problems: (a) employees will erroneously think that management acts arbitrarily, (b) they will
believe the company has a quick trigger finger, or (c) they will
conclude that their own jobs are in jeopardy. These reactions
occur partly because employees typically do not understand
that in the vast majority of instances, management's actions
are not overly hasty but quite the opposite. A California executive once lamented that after a round of layoffs, two of his
best performers quit because they feared their jobs were in
danger. He explained, "Layoff plans had to be kept strictly
confidential per company policy, and I could not tell them
that our restructuring plans did not involve even the possibility of eliminating their positions. Frankly, I would have laid
myself off before them!"

However, too much or careless disclosure can also create post-
termination brainlock. Management terminates an employee
who is unhappy but not desiring revenge. This changes after
she hears that management has been telling her former
coworkers, vendors, and customers what a lousy employee

she was. *Now* she's motivated to sue. The employer not only faces a wrongful-discharge claim, but it may also have to cope with claims of defamation and invasion of privacy.

Therefore, you must strike a balance. A good rule is to disclose the minimum amount of information necessary to avoid speculation. For example, if a senior-level employee has been terminated for conduct involving an affair with his secretary and speculation has been rampant, the lurid details should not be revealed. A statement to employees along these lines would be appropriate: "The vice president's termination followed an investigation into conduct contrary to company policy and values. As a result, we unfortunately found it necessary to terminate his employment."

If an employee has been terminated for repeated performance problems, your goal should be to reassure employees that the boss has not gotten carried away with the at-will rule. If you sense the Law of Employee Speculation rearing its head, you might say to potentially worried employees, "We worked hard with Joe to close the gap between what we needed and what was happening. We eventually had to conclude that the fit was just not right and that Joe needed to move on to a job where he can be more successful."

If a layoff or RIF has just been completed and you see signs that remaining employees may be speculating that they are next, consider an announcement along the following lines: "We have just completed a difficult and painful process. Many good people who contributed to this company are no longer with us. We believe we have now made the necessary reductions to position us for long-term success. There are no guarantees that further reductions won't become necessary, and I know you would want me to be honest with you on this point. Nevertheless, I do believe that with our workforce at its current level, and with your help, we can be successful and not have to go through this process again."

The point is not that you should freely volunteer information about terminated employees. Rather, if you sense the Law of Employee Speculation taking hold, prevent it by calculated, limited disclosure of information. Also, if you do share such information, it's wise to ask for the employees' cooperation in keeping matters confidential out of consideration for the feelings of the terminated employees.

✓ **Tip 3:** During planning for a layoff, share information as widely as possible.

In layoff planning, a number of legal issues typically need to be assessed. These include state or federal notification requirements, potential contract issues, and whether there may be Title VII implications, such as when a layoff disproportionately affects a protected class of employees. Such planning is wise because RIFs, layoffs, and corporate reorganizations often tend to generate claims and litigation.

When it comes to information disclosure, planning seldom extends beyond the cliché of "the less said, the better." Yet, with advice from legal counsel, the employer is almost always better off adopting a weight-forward approach of proactive disclosure. This approach can include newsletters, town hall meetings, and hot lines;

telling employees what management knows; and telling employees what management does not yet know but pledging to inform them once it does. Instead of ducking sensitive questions, management should address them head-on throughout planning and execution. This advice flies in the face of conventional wisdom: that to keep your employees productive and avoid disruption, the company should hold its cards close to the vest and release information only at the last possible moment.

Employers who follow this suggestion may well find that even though it is not, technically speaking, "legal" advice, it's some of the best advice they can follow for keeping their layoffs and the legal system apart. Of my clients who have implemented proactive disclosure plans, none of them have generated a single claim. Instead, among other reactions, reports have come from customers amazed at the good service they received from employees about to lose their jobs. In one situation, there was substantial disagreement among affected employees over the process by which management would determine which employees would be offered jobs at the new facility. Yet the disagreement never reached the level of brainlock because management resisted the temptation to withhold information and shared it instead.

✔ **Tip 4:** Recognize the value of open information flow in all areas of management.

Setting aside workplace claim prevention or claim defense, a number of management experts have faulted American companies for restricted information flow and have recommended erring on the side of disclosure. In his book *Thriving on Chaos*,

Tom Peters exhorts his readers, "With perhaps the exception of confidential personnel records, patent applications, and acquisition information … everything else, including the most confidential of information should, can, and must be shared." To the response that such an approach would make it easier for competitors to learn more, Peters replies that the internal benefits of such disclosure more than offset any potential competitive advantage others might obtain.

Several CEOs lauded by the business community have attributed their success not to a special master plan they brought with them but to a focus on creating an information-rich environment from which ideas would flow. When interviewed about why his company, the Container Store, had for four consecutive years made *Fortune* magazine's annual list of the "100 Best Companies to Work For," CEO Kip Tindell said, "The only way to make people feel they are part of something is to tell them everything."

CEO Gordon Bethune has attributed much of the dramatic turnaround at Continental Airlines to information flow. To change company culture from guarding to sharing information, Bethune employed several tools, including a daily one-page newsletter on what was happening in the organization that day, a weekly recording about company events, and a written test that senior management had to take about every aspect of Continental's business to be eligible for 25 percent of their bonus. Thus, for example, Continental's VP of finance might have to answer questions about the types of engines Continental jets have, and a VP of sales might have to answer questions regarding the

---

Weighing the Benefits of Disclosure
Against Privacy Risks

Although the presumption should be that it's better to disclose, certain types of disclosure do carry legal risks—from common-law
invasion-of-privacy claims to statutory restrictions found in the
Americans with Disabilities Act, the Health Insurance Portability and
Accountability Act, the Immigration Reform and Control Act, and
other federal and some state laws. Moreover, the law of defamation
may rear its head when disclosure harms someone's reputation.
How do you navigate between disclosure and such laws? Use the
following rule of thumb: if the information that might be disclosed
involves an employee's physical or mental health, age, gender, religion, national origin, citizenship, race, sexual orientation, competence, or integrity, consult HR or employment law counsel for
specific advice. Just make sure you do not use an unexamined concern about the law to justify withholding information.

---

company's financial statement. Bethune explained that once
cultural change occurred involving the sharing and flow of
information, ideas sprang forth that led to the company's
turnaround.

These observations and experiences reveal that avoiding the
Sins and practicing the Virtues does much more for a company than protect it from workplace litigation. The benefits
of the Sixth Virtue extend well beyond the legal system to
overall organizational effectiveness.

✓ **Tip 5:** Know the management conditions
        when disclosing information.

Once in a while, practicing the Sixth Virtue backfires. As the
following story illustrates, this backfire typically occurs when
an employer breaks from past practice in an attempt to be
generous in sharing information, yet does so while a culture
of mistrust or hostility toward management still exists.

Information Is Used Against Management

A production manager at a construction company once
accepted the author's advice to give his truck drivers access to
and training on a new computer system. The training
enabled them to know which drivers with what seniority got
which deliveries and when. The manager later angrily
explained that after making this information available, one
driver after another used it to challenge what the company
was doing. Complaints rained down on the hapless manager
from drivers who pointed to the computer screen to support
what they perceived as violations of seniority preference.

Why did this approach go wrong? This well-intentioned
manager was part of a new management group attempting to
change a deeply embedded culture of animosity between
management and two different unions that distrusted each
other as much as management. In such a context, when the
production manager shared this information, it was as if he
had poured gasoline on a fire.

The experience of this construction manager—and of others
who shared information only to see it used as ammunition
against them—does not mean that you should forego the

Sixth Virtue in favor of the Sixth Sin. Rather, it means that when sharing information that will mark a significant break with the past, you should plan carefully. You may need to deliver a "that was then, this is now" message as you identify and focus on the Big Picture, as described in Chapter Eight. Moreover, you may need to do a lot of listening, as discussed in Chapter Seven. With these additional steps, your move from guardian to disseminator of information will succeed, and the new information will spark a positive turn in your relationship with employees.

In the case of the production manager, he worked through the problems, listened to his employees vent, and used conflict-resolution and team-building techniques. Within two months, he had established a level of trust and rapport with his employees unheard of in the company.

Chapter Six Highlights

The Sixth Sin: Letting Employees Speculate

☛ The Law of Employee Speculation means that if employees don't know, they will speculate, and their speculation will always be worse than reality.

☛ In settlement or separation agreements, don't agree to mutual, complete confidentiality clauses. You may need to disclose some information to employees to, for example, dispel the notion that a former employee collected a huge windfall at company expense.

☛ If you do not tell employees why an adverse employment action has been taken against them, they are far more likely to infer unlawful discrimination or retaliation than if you give the reason.

☛ The likelihood that an employee will sue you for wrongful discharge increases exponentially when you don't give a reason for termination.

The Sixth Virtue: Open Information Channels

☛ Generously sharing information enables employees to do their jobs effectively and sends a message of trust and respect.

☛ When it comes to sharing information, the question should not be "Why?" It should be "Why not?"

☛ To determine what to disclose, ask these additional questions: What information do my employees need? What information would I need if I were in their shoes? What information do I need from them? Who needs to be in the loop?

☛ When it comes to sharing information about a termination, tell the employee the reasons for discharge without presenting a detailed bill of particulars. If the person seeks to debate, use the "channeling" technique of helping the employee focus on finding a better fit elsewhere.

☛ As for informing other employees about a discharge, tell them the minimum information you believe is necessary to avoid negative speculation. Then ask for their cooperation in keeping the matter confidential out of respect for the discharged employee.

☛ In layoff planning, resist the conventional wisdom to keep information close to the vest. The opposite approach has served many employers very effectively.

☛ As shown by the experiences of highly successful organizational leaders and management experts, the benefits of practicing the Sixth Virtue go well beyond claim prevention and extend to overall organizational effectiveness.

☛ Certain federal and state laws regulate the disclosure of employee and corporate information. Check with HR and legal counsel to ensure compliance, but avoid the tendency to use an unresearched concern about the law to justify withholding information.

☛ If sharing information will mark a sharp break with your company's culture, you may need to lay groundwork, including delivering a "that was then, this is now" message so that the information is not held against you.

CHAPTER *7*

The Seventh Sin:
Listening Through Your "I"

"A fanatic is one who can't change his mind and won't change the subject."

—Winston Churchill

THE SIN OF LISTENING THROUGH YOUR "I" means letting the manager's perspective or ego dominate all important conversations with employees. Such conversations center only on what the manager understands, desires, or believes and makes no room for what the employees understand, desire, or believe. It means ignoring opportunities to improve work relationships and concomitant productivity. Furthermore, it means eliminating the opportunity to prevent employer-employee relations from spiraling downward, generating brainlock, and dragging the employer into the legal system.

A Disciplinarian Finds Himself on a Path to the Legal System

Joe, the hardest-working crew member, got promoted to supervisor and soon felt frustrated with some former coworkers, particularly Susan. His impatience with her work ethic and attitude reached the point that he decided to give her an oral reprimand. Susan started to explain the problems from her perspective and express frustration with a lack of direction

133

from Joe. But already uncomfortable with this encounter (after all, he got promoted based on his ability to work, not talk) and worried about losing control of the situation, Joe repeatedly cut off Susan's attempts to express her point of view. She lapsed into hostile silence. With coworkers, and later at home, she vented her feelings about her new "idiot" boss.

A pattern quickly set in: dissatisfied supervisor; one-way communication; unhappy employee venting to coworkers, family members, and friends. Reasoning that he had given her every opportunity to improve but she was simply unwilling to do her job, Joe decided to terminate Susan's employment. Susan took this as confirmation that he had it in for her all along, most likely because she was a woman and much older than he. Her spouse, friends, and a few coworkers shared her outrage and encouraged her to seek an attorney. The lawyer noted some of Joe's loose-lipped comments (the Second Sin of Dissin') when he was venting to others ("What the hell is the matter with that woman?" "Why won't she just retire?"). The attorney also found some inconsistencies with company policies and practice (the Fifth Sin of Inconsistency). The lawyer brought a claim based on gender and age discrimination. As a result, Joe's employer lost a potentially productive employee in Susan while gaining a lawsuit that drained precious time, money, and energy from the company and reinforced Joe's already hardening view that you can't trust employees, especially older female ones.

The Seventh Sin of Mismanagement leads managers to talk too much and listen too little. When they do listen, it's only for what they *want* to hear. The results are avoidable mistakes due to erroneous assumptions, excessive interpersonal conflicts, lost opportunities, mistrust, and the inability to resolve problems constructively. Managers such as Joe, who care only about being understood, are in fact not well understood and less able to get what they want from employees.

Why are so many managers led into this sin? One explanation is the Peter Principle—the theory that managers rise to the level of their incompetence. A company promotes employees to managerial positions based on their success in nonmanagerial ones. Some employees, like Joe, succeed in nonsupervisory positions because of their ability to put their nose to the grindstone, block out distractions, and get the job done efficiently. Then they reap the "reward" of being elevated to a position that requires them to coordinate the efforts of others toward shared objectives. Yet the strengths that made them successful at the old job—ability to focus obsessively on individual productivity—actually become obstacles in the new job, which now depends on their ability to communicate with others.

In addition to the Peter Principle, there are three basic reasons why managers commit the Seventh Sin. First, few of us have ever had good role models to teach us. Throughout life we encounter a dearth of good listeners, from parents to teachers to bosses. We're taught that the person in authority primarily does the talking while the person without authority primarily does the listening. When we assume positions of authority, we continue the pattern.

Second, the First Sin discourages us from listening. The instinct to avoid or lean back on skis makes us anxious about what employees might say. We fear losing control of the dialogue or think employees will miss our point if we give them an unfettered opportunity to express their views. We avoid listening as a matter of self-protection.

Third, we are too busy. We already have too much on our plates and cannot afford the extra time to listen to our employees' perspectives. It is a matter of triage and, frankly, that patient can wait. Our customers, bosses, and paperwork take priority.

The three basic reasons lead to three basic listening models:

Model 1: The Toe-Tapper.
This type of manager defines listening as "waiting to talk." When employees speak, the manager looks upon them as if she were sitting in a dentist's chair: when, oh when, will they finish? This type of listener is guilty of the Second Sin, of dissin'. The manager's impatience about listening effectively disregards the employees' point of view. To test this point at home, pair up family members at the dinner table. Have one member of the pair speak to the other on a subject of importance to her while the other member consciously avoids listening—looks away, talks to others at the table, plays with food, etc. Even knowing that the exercise is artificial, the speaker will invariably feel annoyed.

Model 2: The Autobiographer.
This type of manager treats employees as objects in his ongoing autobiographical masterpiece. Whatever they say serves as an opportunity for him to place their comments in the

context of *his* experiences, beliefs, or points of view. Supervisor to employee, interrupting her: "Wait, Susan, here's what I did when I had that job before my promotion and what made me department leader in production."

Model 3: The Cross-Examiner.

This type of manager resembles defense counsel grilling an employee who has sued her former employer. The cross-examining attorney listens carefully to the plaintiff. However, the purpose is not to understand but to pounce, to find weaknesses that can be exploited to destroy the employee's case, credibility, or both. Sadly, some managers seem to cross-examine an employee to highlight the employee's faults and mistakes while simultaneously proving their superiority. Yet it is hard to imagine a worse model than a courtroom for running a workplace. Such managers may prove their superiority—but at a huge cost in morale, retention, productivity, and generation of brainlock.

The Seventh Virtue:
Listening Through Your Ears

"God gave you a hint with a gift of one mouth and two ears."
—Yiddish saying

THE SEVENTH VIRTUE MEANS OBTAINING a clear picture of where employees stand, understanding *their* perspectives, ideas, and beliefs—even if this means temporarily suspending the manager's own preconceptions. Practicing this Virtue does not mean abandoning control or direction; it means solidifying trust and understanding while enhancing the manager's leadership role. It means communicating so that the toughest possible workplace subjects can be addressed without generating brainlock and a trip to the legal system.

The Disciplinarian Learns to Listen

Return to the story of Joe and Susan, this time substituting the Seventh Virtue for the Seventh Sin. As in the first story, Joe gets promoted and observes that some of his former coworkers, most notably Susan, do not perform at acceptable levels. He decides to address the expectations gap by applying lessons from the new-manager training program he has been attending. This time he counters the instinct to avoid listening by making a conscious effort to hear Susan's perspective. In this way, Joe applies the best and most constructive form of discipline. He seeks to *learn*. (The word "discipline" actually derives from the Latin "discipulus," which means "pupil" and from "discere," meaning "to learn.")

Instead of cutting off Susan's explanations, he invites them. He asks questions designed to elicit whether Susan understands workplace expectations; is prepared to close the performance gap; and perceives any obstacles, such as systemic workplace conditions, a lack of training, or something Joe does that contributes to her problem. By affirmatively eliciting this information from Susan, Joe creates the greatest likelihood for successful gap closure. Misconceptions and erroneous assumptions get corrected. Even though Susan receives a difficult message, she feels respected. In this way, Joe creates optimal conditions for either (a) reversing a negative behavior pattern and creating a positive, productive relationship; or (b) determining that the fit between Susan and the job is not right and making a change without generating brainlock.

The Benefits of Virtuous Managing

Practicing the Seventh Virtue provides two great benefits, *informational* and *emotional*.

Benefit 1: The Informational Benefit.

When managers do not listen to employees as a means to learn and understand, they typically rely on assumptions. However, these assumptions often prove erroneous, which causes opportunities to be lost and solvable problems to remain unsolved. By employing affirmative listening techniques, you can replace assumptions with truth. To put it another way, by avoiding passive reliance on conjecture, you avoid making of yourself the first three letters of the word "assumption."

Legal Nugget

Listening During Internal Investigations

To keep an investigation of an internal employee complaint from ending up in court, an important but often overlooked element is the ability of the person conducting the investigation to listen. By concentrating on understanding the complainant, the accused, and the witnesses, and by using listening techniques such as those described below, the investigator will help ensure the soundness of the investigation and create the best possible conditions for the parties accepting the findings and corrective action plan. Even when one or more parties continues to see things differently, they feel like they were heard. Brainlock typically does not set in, and the internal investigation helps prevent subsequent litigation.

Some workplace relationships are bound to fail. Not every employee-to-job match fits. However, numerous failed relationships could be saved. One culprit in such preventable failures: mistaken assumptions. The supervisor assumes something about the employee's abilities, attitude, or work ethic that may be somewhat true but is not entirely accurate. Conversely, the employee assumes something about the supervisor that likewise has some truth but is not entirely accurate. Yet if the parties honestly explored each other's positions, they would discover that their respective assumptions reinforced erroneous views and blocked an understanding upon which they could have built a positive work relationship.

The "Negligent" Typist

The late management expert W. Edwards Deming gave an example of erroneous assumptions when discussing the distinction between "common causes" (systemic reasons for workplace behaviors or results) and "special causes" (such as variations in individual worker actions). The first half of the twentieth century saw the proliferation of typing pools, in which women sat at workstations typing large volumes of documents. As recounted by Rafael Aguayo in *Dr. Deming: the American Who Taught the Japanese about Quality*, the typing pool in Deming's example maintained statistical controls involving words per minute (quantity) and errors per page (quality). Falling outside statistical standards prompted management to initiate progressive discipline, which could eventually lead to the typist's termination.

On one occasion, before administering discipline, management asked an employee why she was having trouble meeting statistical controls. She replied that when the afternoon sun came through a nearby window, it created a glare that caused her to squint. Sure enough, after management adjusted her workstation, her quality and quantity returned to statistically acceptable levels. According to Deming, this demonstrated that the cause of the problem was "common" (work environment), not "specific" (incompetent employee), as initially thought. To look at it another way, this story shows the value of management substituting inquiry for assumptions about an employee problem.

Benefit 2: The Emotional Benefit.

One's employment is not an exclusive left-brain endeavor. How you manage employee feelings may be more indicative of success than how you manage employee thoughts.

Listening from the employee's perspective provides tremendous emotional value in the workplace. Leadership expert Stephen R. Covey speaks of this type of listening as "healing," like giving oxygen to people who desperately need it. When you listen to employees in order to understand them, they become more inclined to follow your direction, meet your expectations, and accept changes or decisions with which they may not agree or even like.

Tools and Techniques

Here are six useful tools to help avoid the Seventh Sin. Although they are designed for the workplace, try practicing them at home. Listening effectively to a spouse, parents, children, siblings, or significant others will produce inestimable benefits. Besides, family time presents practice opportunities. In addition to reaping potentially life-changing personal benefits, being able to apply these techniques in the home—with its greater emotional history (or baggage)—means you can apply them anywhere.

✓ **Tip 1:** Take a two-for-one
approach.

A simple but highly useful listening technique is to take to heart God's hint about one mouth and two ears. For every statement you make, ask at least two questions. When orienting new employees to company policy and expectations, liberally mix in questions regarding what they perceive or understand. Before discussing an employee's performance, think of questions concerning the person's accomplishments, failures, goals, challenges, and opportunities. Even when confronting an employee for inappropriate behavior, include questions regarding the employee's understanding of what does or does not constitute acceptable conduct in the workplace.

Whatever your actual question-to-statement percentage works out to be, if you consciously apply the two-for-one approach, you will be in listening mode even when conveying the most forceful of messages. It will induce you to think of questions ahead of time since the best way to work the percentages is to start the dialogue by asking questions. Give the two-for-one a try. You might say it comes highly recommended.

✔ **Tip 2:** The
E-A-R.

As described in Ken Blanchard's audio program *Personal Excellence*, E-A-R is an acronym for Explore, Acknowledge, and Respond. You begin by *exploring* the employee's views, issues, or problems, saying, "Tell me what's on your mind." "Explain your view of the matter." "Give me details or examples of what you mean." After exploring the employee's position, you *acknowledge* by confirming the central themes or salient points of what the employee has just said. A useful trigger for remembering to acknowledge is to begin by saying the employee's name: "Tyler, it sounds like these are your concerns…."

Only after exploring and acknowledging do you *respond* with your own view. In this way, you obtain potentially valuable information, avoid mistaken assumptions, and score important emotional points. All of these activities combine to increase the effectiveness of your response and the likelihood the employee will accept it.

✓ Tip 3: Funnel your decision making.

Visualize this method by picturing a funnel. At the top or wide end, you pour in the employee's information using broad, open-ended questions. Next, filter the information through the bottom or narrow end of the funnel by asking the employee, "Do I understand you correctly that …?" Then summarize what you think the *employee thinks* are the key points of his message.

✓ Tip 4: Channel a discussion with directive listening.

How do you make yourself listen when you must get certain points across but time is limited or you face an employee who's a walking filibuster? When you simply have no time at the moment to listen, employ the dismiss-and-redirect tool discussed in Chapter Three. Tell the employee the matter is too important to handle when you're distracted but you want to meet to discuss it at a specific future time.

To head off an incessant talker, you can listen using directive questions. Essentially, you control the dialogue and even interrupt the employee as necessary, but you do so with questions designed to direct the discussion to where it needs to be. Using the person's name can help: "Now Kris, I want to ask you about something else…." "Bobby, I understand your concerns about employees you think are getting special treatment, but I need to ask you right now what you think needs to happen to achieve the goal of your arriving at work by 8:00 a.m. every day?" "Taylor, let's talk about those monthly sales call reports. What is your view about the issue of timeliness and the need for sufficient detail, and what steps do you see taking?"

You could of course direct employees in such situations through statements or commands. Yet, by doing it through questions, you accomplish the same result without being overbearing, and you give the employees a greater sense of participation. The employees will therefore be more receptive and more likely to take responsibility for the issue under discussion.

✓ **Tip 5:** Become a Monk.

The "Monk" method of listening is especially useful for handling heated discussions. It comes from a rule of discourse used in an ancient European monastery. Because ecclesiastical discussions often became emotional, a rule was established that before one monk could contradict another, he first had to summarize and confirm the other's position. For example, Monk A might opine that Goliath was a tragic victim of biblical discrimination against big people. No matter how nonsensical Monk B considered this view to be, he first had to summarize it and confirm the accuracy of his understanding with Monk A before asserting a contrary view.

This method may seem cumbersome. However, establishing it as an agreed-upon rule before proceeding can greatly lower the temperature of an emotional debate. Hearing your views summarized and confirmed by your opponent reduces the hostility level and makes you less resistant to an opposing viewpoint. Even when you don't make the Monk's technique an agreed-upon rule, you can practice it yourself as you weigh in on a heated discussion.

✓ **Tip 6:** The Triple
       Two.

This technique stems from a *Wall Street Journal* article discussing a corporate CEO's method of obtaining a reality check and overcoming his subordinates' reluctance to speak candidly to him. He periodically asks subordinates three two-part questions: (1) What two things am I currently doing that should I stop doing? (2) What two things should I continue doing? (3) What two things should I start doing?

Although this technique was designed by the corporate "emperor" to ensure that he was wearing clothes, you and your employees can use it at all organizational levels, regardless of reporting relationship. Whether you elicit more or less than two suggestions per question does not matter; you will receive valuable information and reap important emotional benefits by showing a desire to hear the other person's perspective—even when it stings a bit.

Whichever listening technique you choose, beware the common tendency to start in listening mode but shift quickly to manager-as-speaker mode, as when you ignore the A in E-A-R or the narrow end of the funnel. The following story provides a typical example of a manager who thinks he is practicing the Seventh Virtue when he really isn't.

Making an Unhappy Hostess More Unhappy

After teaching these listening techniques to a group of restaurant managers, the author received some negative feedback about the tools' effectiveness. A manager complained that applying the Seventh Virtue to an emotional encounter with a hostess only made things worse.

On one stressful night, the manager was already scrambling when he had to deal with the tearful hostess after a patron did not get desired seating at the desired time and took it out on her. As the manager explained, he initiated a discussion with his employee by asking open-ended questions. However, as he related the remainder of their discussion, it became evident that he failed to ask if he understood her and neglected to summarize her key points from her frame of reference before saying what he thought should happen. By skipping the *acknowledge* step of the E-A-R method and going immediately to *respond*, he misunderstood something about her response to the angry customer. His resulting misperception only intensified her hurt feelings and confirmed in her mind that he was taking the customer's side. As this manager's experience attests, the Seventh Virtue can backfire when you don't practice both listening and confirming. However, if you're aware of this tendency, making a conscious effort and some practice will produce good results.

Chapter Seven Highlights

The Seventh Sin: Listening Through Your "I"

☛ This sin means hearing only your own perspective, not that of your employees. Managers often avoid listening from fear of hearing unpleasant news, losing authority, or wasting time.

☛ When you fail to invest in your employees by listening to them, all of you spend more time in a problem-solving mode than a growth or development mode.

☛ Poor listeners miss opportunities to prevent claims and instead increase the likelihood of brainlock.

☛ Managers who are poor listeners often fit into these categories:
  - *The Toe-Tapper*, who thinks that listening means waiting to talk.
  - *The Autobiographer*, who translates everything into his or her own experiences and beliefs.
  - *The Cross-Examiner*, who listens for an employee's mistakes or weaknesses.

The Seventh Virtue: Listening Through Your Ears

☛ Embracing this virtue does not mean abdicating authority or control; rather, it makes the manager's leadership more effective.

☛ This virtue has two continuous benefits:

- *Informational benefits*, which help you acquire valuable insights and avoid mistaken assumptions.
- *Emotional benefits*, which help you effectively manage the "feelings" aspect of workplace relationships.

☛ Six techniques will help you:

- *Two-for-one, or "God's hint."* For every one statement you make, ask two questions.
- *The E-A-R, or Explore, Acknowledge, Respond.* Explore the employee's views or perspective, Acknowledge what the employee has said, then (and only then) Respond.
- *The funnel.* Pour the employee's story into the wide-end of the funnel through open-ended questions. Then sift out the essence of the communication through the narrow end by asking, "Do I understand you correctly?" and summarizing *the employee's* key points.
- *Directive listening.* Control and even interrupt overly talkative employees with questions that lead them to the subject, "Okay, Sam, now I need to ask you about …."
- *The Monk.* Before you disagree with someone's position, summarize it and confirm your understanding. Then express your opposing view.
- *The Triple Two.* Ask employees to answer this question: What two things should I (a) stop doing, (b) continue doing, or (c) start doing?

☛ Beware the tendency to begin in good listening mode but shift unwittingly into manager-as-speaker.

☛ Practice these techniques at home.

CHAPTER 8

The Eighth Sin:
Front-of-the-Nose Perspective

"Where there is no vision, the people perish."

—Proverbs 29:18

HAVING A FRONT-OF-THE-NOSE PERSPECTIVE means getting caught up in day-to-day or moment-to-moment issues, events, or crises. It means spending most of your time and energy reacting to what's right in front of you without thinking about—much less linking what you're doing to—mission, vision, values, or goals. Instead of planning, communicating, and acting in terms of the forest, you fight fires tree by tree.

The Failed Company Retreat

A health food company that generated millions of dollars in international sales planned a retreat for senior executives and board members to address and—everyone hoped—resolve organizational problems regarding direction and culture. But at one point during the retreat, the red-faced VP of international sales yelled and gestured at the VP of production, who sat back in his chair, glowering. The sales VP had just returned from Europe, where he had met with outraged distributors whom the company had failed to supply with products to sell.

Unbeknownst to the sales VP, the CEO and CFO had previously met with the production VP about excessive inventory—specifically, having to destroy products that exceeded their shelf life. They pointedly reminded him that appropriate inventory levels would be an important factor in calculating his annual bonus. The production VP reacted by tightening up production, which set off a chain reaction that eventually led to the explosion of emotion at the company retreat.

It turned out that the responsible executives—the CEO, CFO, the production VP, *and* the sales VP—had never collectively addressed what the appropriate inventory balance would be. Each executive maintained a front-of-the-nose perspective, unwittingly setting in motion a chain of events leading to hundreds of thousands of dollars in lost revenue, a serious erosion of good will with distributors, and smoldering hostility and distrust among key members of the company's executive team.

The relentless press of the moment and of immediate goals often prevents managers from focusing on the organization's Big Picture. Investment in relationships with subordinates, superiors, and colleagues gets blocked. Opportunities are lost. Problems remain unresolved. The collective sense of mission fails to emerge.

The Eighth Sin also tends to foster climates in which employees assert claims. Lacking a Big Picture focus, a sense of purpose, or an awareness of why things matter, employees tend to fill in the gaps with negative assumptions and speculation that can start them on the path to brainlock. Managers' front-of-the-nose perspective makes them more error-prone, more apt to be inconsistent or commit other Sins. They fail to put the issue, problem, or challenge into a broader, longer-term context and instead simply react to the moment.

When claims are made, the Eighth Sin creates problems in claim defense. The difference between a favorable or adverse finding may well depend on whether the employer's action, such as firing an employee, comes off as a hasty, ill-considered reaction or a thought-through decision tied to important company policies, values, goals, or mission. Management should be able to identify and articulate the relevant goals, values, or mission so that the connection between them and the adverse employment action can be shown. Otherwise, there is a risk that the termination decision will be viewed as an emotional reaction and dangerous speculation will arise that unlawful ulterior motives (such as race, gender or age bias) played a part.

When you and your organization get stuck in a front-of-the-nose perspective, you suffer a number of adverse effects:

Effect 1: Excessive stress.

Ceaselessly fighting fires is highly taxing and may create a feeling of emptiness as you wonder, Is this all there is? Moreover, stress can lead to solving only the most superficial problems; though you may temporarily extinguish some flames, the embers smolder, ready to rekindle at the first opportunity.

Avoid a Front-of-the-Nose Perspective in Dealing with the EEOC

All too often, U.S. employers receive notices from the Equal Employment Opportunity Commission and state anti-discrimination agencies that former or current employees have asserted claims of discrimination, harassment, or retaliation. The agency demands a response. Many employers respond from a front-of-the-nose perspective and don't consider what course of action is best overall. Annoyed, anxious, or aggravated, they respond peremptorily that the claim is baseless and they shouldn't be bothered with something so ridiculous. To an agency investigator overloaded with active files, these employers can appear to be arrogant abusers of power and privilege who deserve to be brought down a peg or two. Employer, employee, and agency often begin the downward spiral to the legal system.

Instead of reacting like this, employers should start by identifying goals. These involve answering questions such as (1) How do we resolve this claim at the earliest practical time, without having to go to court? (2) If we made a mistake, what can we do to correct it at the earliest opportunity while minimizing the consequences? (3) How do we best persuade the agency that we did not violate the law and that our decisions tie in to the company's legitimate mission, goals, policies, or values? (4) What can we learn from this process that will help us improve our HR, management, and claim-prevention practices?

Oriented with such questions, the employer can make intelligent, cost-effective choices, often beginning with whether to mediate the claim. (The EEOC and most state agencies now promote mediation.) The opportunity for early mediation is often over-looked by employers with a front-of-the-nose perspective. Yet in all probability, this is when and how the claim can be settled at the cheapest overall price. Early mediation can be especially helpful if mistakes were made and management wants to correct the problem before the stakes escalate. Even if mediation does not produce a settlement, the employer will have gained valuable information about the details of the claim. This information will help organize, articulate, and support a position designed to per-suade the agency investigator that the claim lacks merit. A favor-able agency finding does not guarantee that no litigation will ensue. However, a favorable finding will end the matter in most cases because plaintiffs' attorneys frequently use the agency finding as a litmus test of litigation-worthiness. The employer can then move on to the fourth question and identify steps for improvement, as discussed in Chapter Five on the litigation post-mortem.

Effect 2: Inefficiency.

Without a Big Picture focus, departments, managers, and employees concentrate only on what they need in their little corner of universe. They don't identify—much less imple-ment—ideas for overall organizational improvement. The parts of the company work against each other, instead of together, and a great level of effort does not bring great results. In organizational terms, this phenomenon is called suboptimization. Because no one is focusing on the Big Picture, the company fails to optimize its parts and the whole becomes substantially less than the sum of its parts.

Effect 3: Ineffective, even counterproductive, management training.

Because there is no consensus about what professional development programs should achieve, transfer of training (moving from lessons to actual workplace behavior) cannot occur. Instead, managers simply feel more stressed when they're pulled away from their firefighting duties to attend useless classes.

Effect 4: A horse-and-buggy problem.

A narrow focus also prevents you from preparing for major changes in markets, industry, technology, or demographics. Even if you were the best buggy maker in the world in 1890, without a Big Picture focus you would lack the perspective to think of your company as the best transportation company whose principal current product happens to be based on the horse-and-buggy mode of travel. As a result, within a generation, your stock would be worth horse manure.

The Eighth Virtue:
The Big Picture

"Of all the things I've done, the most vital is coordinating the talents of those who work for us and pointing them toward a certain goal."

—Walt Disney

THE EIGHTH VIRTUE means aligning ideas, actions, and decisions with the organization's mission, vision, values, and goals. The Big Picture becomes a *picture frame* to put around relationships with employees. Job status, expectations, growth, change, and accountability get placed within the frame and stay connected to what is centrally important.

Navigating an EEO Minefield

A white male accounting supervisor experienced continual problems with his "two underperforming malcontents." He wished to fire them, but one was Hispanic, the other was African-American, both were female, and he was afraid of being sued. He tried getting through each day by ignoring them as much as possible (in contrast to his treatment of the other, white, employees whom he liked and respected). From time to time, he would become sufficiently frustrated at their misdeeds to vent his feelings, which invariably provoked a counterattack that he was unfair and favored the white employees over them. The supervisor would then get fearful of legal action and back off by, for example, marking performance evaluations as "acceptable" when they weren't, failing to implement disciplinary action in accordance with company policy, and otherwise failing to confront the problems or attempt to understand his employees' views. The supervisor blamed politically correct times for his inability to manage.

Then one day the supervisor attended a management training program with the HR director. With coaching from the latter, and desperate enough to risk change, he embarked on an entirely new approach to dealing with his employees, beginning with the Eighth Virtue. He identified five fundamental standards that connected his department to the company's mission. Next, he met with all of his six direct reports to discuss their work and his expectations in relation to the five standards. He set up follow-up meetings every thirty days and established a practice of confirming each meeting's critical points in memos to the employees.

Results? Greatly surprised, the supervisor reported that the four employees with no performance problems actually got better. After the Hispanic employee responded with skepticism and hostility, the supervisor calmly repeated that his goal was not to fire her but to ensure the success of the department and all of its employees, including her. Later he held a disciplinary meeting with her for failure to meet one of the standards—office professionalism and mutual respect—after she reduced the black employee to tears by accusing her of being a turncoat after the latter expressed support for the boss's new approach.

Although the Hispanic employee labeled the new management approach a ruse to get her terminated and threatened legal action, it soon became evident that the legal system no longer provided leverage. To her threats of litigation, the manager responded that she was certainly entitled to seek legal counsel and assert claims; however, she still had to conform to the five standards, including treating others with respect. She soon backed away from her threats of legal action and quietly left the company a few months later. As for the African-American employee (whom the supervisor had once described as "the greater of the two evils"), their relationship improved dramatically. Two years later, when she tendered her resignation to attend to some personal issues, the manager lobbied strenuously that an exception be made to company policy to give her a leave of absence even though she did not meet the criteria. The HR director then reminded him of the Big Picture, including avoiding the Fifth Sin of Inconsistency. She advised him to look instead for opportunities to re-employ her in the future.

The Benefits of Virtuous Managing

The story of the accounting supervisor illustrates not only the workplace benefits of practicing the Eighth Virtue but also how management can extricate itself from sticky legal situations. Risks arise when a white male supervisor takes disciplinary action against two females who are the only minorities in his department. However, the legal momentum shifted completely once the supervisor (a) identified and articulated the Big Picture—the five critical departmental standards, (b) connected his performance and conduct expectations to them, (c) communicated this connection orally and in writing, and (d) used the same approach with all of his employees. The supervisor's relentless focus on the Big Picture cut through the legal risks that arise when tough decisions need to be made and manager and employee differ markedly by age, race, gender, or other legally protected classification.

This story also shows how a Big Picture focus can unite a diverse workforce. Protected-class differences often promote more distrust than synergy. But a workplace centered on high expectations and the Big Picture will tend to minimize distrust and promote synergy because there is neither the time nor inclination to speculate on ulterior motives or stereotypes. Instead, the emphasis is on contribution. Synergy can then come from diversity as employees of different races, creeds, origins, ages, and backgrounds contribute their respective talents, skills, and insights toward realization of shared objectives.

While the Eighth Sin, or front-of-the-nose perspective, tends to encourage commission of the other Seven Sins, the Eighth Virtue similarly promotes practicing the other Seven Virtues. By committing to the Big Picture, you will naturally find your weight going forward on your skis. You see the necessity of being proactive and taking initiative, of confronting problems and pursuing opportunities at the earliest stages, of addressing the very things most managers would be most apt to avoid. The Big Picture gives you the confidence to ski challenging terrain; be direct, specific, and honest; maintain a strong E-R-A; keep your ducks in a row; open information channels; and listen as you seek ways of pursing the mission and accomplishing the goals. The Eighth Virtue is truly a bonus, in that starting with the Big Picture generates positive momentum in all aspects of employee relations.

Tools and Techniques

The Big Picture benefits organizations in numerous important ways. Here are a few tips on how to make the most of those benefits.

✔ **Tip 1:** Put the "why"
         in your communications.

Before communicating with your employees anything of importance pertaining to their performance, first ask yourself, "Why?" In terms of the Big Picture, why are you about to give employees direction or feedback as to expected performance, attendance, or conduct? After answering this question, include the reason in your communication to employees. Putting the "why" into the communication process will go a long way toward promoting acceptance of your message and aligning employees with the Big Picture. This will be especially true with your younger employees for whom, in contrast to older generations, being told what to do is not enough. They also want to know why.

✔ **Tip 2:** Identify the
         Big Picture.

Assuming you commit to focusing on the Big Picture, what steps should you take to identify it? The following questions will help.

- What is the mission of your company (defined as the essential reasons for its existence)?
- What is the vision of your company (defined as a compelling image of a desired future)?
- What are the company's fundamental values?

- What are the company's short- and long-term goals?
- Considering your answers to the first four questions and your role as a member of the company's management team, what are *your* (a) mission, (b) vision, (c) core values, and (d) short- and long-term goals?
- With respect to your employees, (a) what do you need from them in order to achieve the Big Picture, (b) what are *their* goals, and (c) how can you help them accomplish those goals?

✓ Tip 3: Write a Big Picture outline.

If you are a serious Big Picture proponent, the effort to identify mission, vision, values, and goals is not complete until you have reduced them to the written word. The likelihood that you will accomplish your goals increases dramatically when you put them in writing and use the written description as a baseline for charting progress. Not only will such a document prove helpful in accomplishing Big Picture objectives, but it will also serve as a continual prompt for putting the Big Picture frame around everything significant in manager-employee communications.

A useful tool is the Big Picture outline. It starts with a statement of your short- and long-term goals, as identified in Tip 2. It includes what you desire to accomplish and goes further to cover timetables for accomplishing the goals and measuring progress along the way. List the steps for getting there, including resources you need, potential obstacles, and benchmarks or other measuring sticks. The more specific you make the outline, the more effective it will be. This document will serve as your personal management blueprint. It will lead to discussions, follow-up memos, and other outlines or revisions as you continue to communicate the vision and your employees' role in helping to achieve it. (For model documents to help you define the Big Picture, articulate your commitment, and more, see the Appendix at the end of this book.)

✔ **Tip 4:** Create a Star Profile

For Big Picture managers, a great tool is the Star Profile, derived from a concept of Lou Adler. Unlike a job description, which lists minimum requirements and responsibilities, this Profile succinctly describes what a *star* employee would do. One way to create a Star Profile is to sit in a comfortable chair, close your eyes, and visualize a movie playing in your head. It stars the kind of employee who's a joy to manage. Envision important things about the job—performance, attendance, conduct—that the employee does consistently. Now, in simple sentences, list each thing you see in the movie that's important and that makes you smile. Focus the profile to make it short (less than a page), simple, and clear. For the construction workers who report to you, perhaps one line says, "Hard hat always on in construction areas." For the salesperson, perhaps, "Pursues every lead at the earliest opportunity." For a truck driver, "Doesn't just dump the load; makes the customer feel he personally cares about on-time delivery." For a VP of finance, "Thinks not only about where we can save money but where we should *spend* to achieve our goal of doubling sales revenue within five years."

The Star Profile can be used to communicate E-R-A and evaluate your employees' alignment with the Big Picture. It doesn't supplant a performance appraisal system but can be used in connection with it to help give employees meaningful feedback as to how they're truly doing in your eyes. The Star Profile is not a "pie in the sky" wish list that cannot possibly be met. You shouldn't necessarily expect—and in fact may never manage—an employee who nails each thing on the list. You probably wouldn't achieve every aspect of a Star Profile of your *own* job. Nevertheless, if you take the trouble to develop a Star Profile, you will find that the quality of the direction you give your employees will improve. They will have a better sense of the path to success. And you will be better able to make tough calls about employees who really don't fit and act without creating brainlock.

✔ **Tip 5:** Use the Big Picture to communicate HR's contribution.

If you're a manager in human resources, you can improve and emphasize HR's value to your organization by zeroing in on the Big Picture and how HR can help realize it. Such a focus will show that the human resources department is genuinely a *resource* for achieving the organization's mission, vision, and goals. For example, let's say that in a meeting, the CFO points to the largest slice on the cost pie chart and notes that employee wages and benefits make up 72 percent of total company expenditures. Follow up with her after the meeting on the importance of getting the greatest possible return on that huge 72 percent investment and on how HR can help achieve that return.

By the same token, when coaching managers on employee problems, get them to focus on the Big Picture the way the accounting supervisor did. Ask them Big Picture questions and have them describe the employee problem in terms of what the *managers* consider fundamentally important. Coaching in this fashion will not only improve effectiveness but also engender trust. Managers in production, operations, sales, marketing, R&D, or finance who receive such coaching will see how HR contributes to bottom-line organizational effectiveness.

✔ **Tip 6:** Use the Campfire Technique
           to manage your boss.

Several couples went on a camping trip in the mountains. After dinner, the women took a moonlit walk to observe the constellations. The men stayed by the campfire to smoke cigars, pass around bottles labeled with men's first names, and otherwise engage in man-like behavior. Unexpectedly, a serious discussion broke out. One of the men vented his frustration about his boss's micromanaging, over-controlling nature. Another member of the group responded that he had managed to avoid such experiences throughout his career thanks to a simple technique. "Whenever I begin with a new boss, I ask him what his goals are. The boss usually just stares at me with a blank look on his face, since no one ever asked him this question before."

This campfire companion explained that using this question and being guided by the answer results in almost total freedom—even with micromanagers. Ironically, and as others have discovered, expressing interest in the boss's goals does not put the employee more squarely under the boss's thumb; rather, it results in greater freedom. Why? Because such bosses tend to view employees as so many cats they're forced to herd. When one of the "cats" stuns them by expressing interest in the bosses' goals or agenda, they think, "Finally! An employee I can actually trust!" This approach is not just a useful tool for increased freedom from a controlling boss; it's also a great way to achieve a positive, constructive, and mutually respectful relationship with any supervisor. All you have to do is express interest in understanding the boss's Big Picture. Call it the Campfire Technique.

Chapter Eight Highlights

The Eighth Sin: Front-of-the-Nose Perspective

☞ This means being slave to the moment—to e-mail, voicemail, the person in your doorway, whatever clamors for attention.

☞ It means remaining stuck in a firefighting mode as opposed to exploring opportunities or investing in relationships.

☞ A front-of-the-nose perspective tends to generate brain-lock and increase the risk of workplace claims. It also makes defending employment decisions difficult since they are more likely to appear arbitrary and infected with illegal biases.

☞ A front-of-the-nose perspective increases workplace stress and promotes inefficiency as the whole becomes less than the sum of its parts.

☞ Training does not transfer; lessons are lost in the crush of day-to-day pressures before the new ideas can work their way into managerial behavior.

☞ Avoid a narrow, react-to-the-moment approach in responding to claims before agencies such as the EEOC. At the outset, focus on how you can resolve the claim at the earliest practical time, including fixing any mistakes you may have made, figuring out how you can best persuade the agency that your actions were entirely lawful, and exploring what you can learn to improve HR and management practices.

The Eighth Virtue: The Big Picture

☛ Identify the Big Picture and use it as a picture frame to place around your relationship with your employees.

☛ When addressing expectations, status, and growth potential with employees, relate these to the Big Picture.

☛ A Big Picture focus not only allows managers to manage diverse employees without fear of discrimination claims, but it also creates an environment in which diversity leads to synergy.

☛ Today's employee needs to know *why*, not just *what* or *how*.

☛ The Eighth Virtue is a bonus because practicing it naturally inclines you toward practice of the other Seven Virtues.

☛ Identify the mission, vision, fundamental values, and goals of your organization. Ask the same questions about these of yourself and your employees.

☛ Use a written Big Picture outline to identify the desired goals and your steps and timetables for achieving them.

☛ Create a Star Profile. List the critical things a star employee would actually do. Use the profile to communicate expectations to employees and assess their alignment with the Big Picture.

☛ Show how HR is a resource that helps direct the human beings employed to achieve the organization's Big Picture mission, vision, and goals.

☛ Use the Campfire Technique with your boss. Ask about the boss's own goals or Big Picture. The result will be a more constructive relationship as well as more autonomy for you to get your job done.

CHAPTER 9

Moving from Sin to Virtue

"We are what we repeatedly do. Excellence, therefore, is not an act but a habit."

— Shaquille O'Neal (quoting Aristotle)

BOOKS LIKE THIS ONE OFTEN OCCUPY the same niche as fad diets. They make sense, sound persuasive, and will produce beneficial results if applied. Yet all too often, they fade from consciousness before being converted into action. They end up gathering dust on the shelf, next to the manual that was supposed to have tucked in your belly and slimmed down your hips.

In an attempt to combat this phenomenon, this book does not end with a description of the Sins and Virtues and an exhortation to move from one to the other. Instead, it concludes with tools, techniques, and examples culled from research, observation, and experience regarding the concept of transfer of training. Transfer of training involves converting thought into action, taking the lessons out of the classroom and into actual workplace behavior, practice, and habit. For readers ready to move from contemplation of change to real change, this chapter provides the means to do so, both on the individual level and on the organizational level. If you want to shift your weight forward on your skis, here's how to do it.

Individual Strategies

Moving from Sins to Virtues means that you as a manager must learn and apply new behaviors and approaches, using the beginning-skier instinct to your advantage and committing to positive change. Each time you substitute a Virtue when you otherwise would have committed a Sin, you experience its benefits. When, through repetition, this substitution becomes *habit*, you move into the rank of virtuoso managers.

A Manager Ready for Change

Cheryl received little management, leadership, or communications training after her promotion at a real estate development company. She was promoted based on her intelligence, experience, and hard work—not her interpersonal skills. She found managing employees to be the least pleasant part of her job; she much preferred interacting with customers or developing projects on her own. Her relationship with subordinates could best be described as mutual toleration dotted with occasionally blowups.

During a training program, Cheryl identified strongly with each of the Sins—the instinct to avoid by leaning back on skis, dissin', rationalizing, and on down the list. This recognition, combined with a lot of pent-up career frustration, led Cheryl beyond contemplating change to developing a plan. She identified the points in the training that applied most to her and committed to implementing them. She set specific goals, such as using the two-for-one method in listening to each employee at least once a week and giving each at least one written positive D-I-S per month. She started keeping a journal of goals, steps, and progress. In addition, she periodically scheduled feedback sessions using the Triple Two technique to assess whether her employees shared her perceptions about the changes.

Cheryl's individual plan succeeded not only with her subordinates, who responded enthusiastically to the changes, but also with company executives, who were impressed. Within six months, Cheryl received a promotion to a director-level position in the company.

Tools and Techniques

Cheryl's story shows that even on their own, managers can make a perceptible, positive difference through a commitment and a plan. The following tips have helped managers make the journey from Sin to Virtue.

✓ **Tip 1:** Use the self-protective instinct to advantage.

Up to now it has seemed that the instinct to avoid was always the manager's nemesis. The natural desire to protect yourself induces you to put weight back on skis and avoid a problem just when you most need to do the opposite. Yet it's possible to convert this instinct to good use. It can serve as a wake-up call that there is an issue you need to address, a problem you need to solve, or an opportunity you need to pursue. The little voice inside you whispering, "Avoid this one," "Wait and see," or "Let someone else handle it" gets translated into

"This one needs to be dealt with now," "Own it," or "Put together a game plan and execute it."

Think back to Sally, the department manager described in Chapter One. When she returned from her Colorado ski trip to another episode of Kevin's complaining and resistance to the new computer system, her natural instinct was to avoid an aggressive employee. Instead, however, after she learned the connection between the beginning-skier instinct and the workplace, Sally applied what she learned on the ski slope. She used the instinct as a trigger to do the opposite—in this case, to hold a meeting with Kevin promptly and communicate her expectations of his workplace behavior. In this way, the inclination toward Sin served to prompt virtuous action.

✔ **Tip 2:** Make a commitment.

During World War II, U.S. government officials met with groups of housewives to urge them to conserve resources in those lean times by serving their families not only the traditionally consumed parts of beef cattle but also the internal organs—kidneys, livers, pancreases, brains, etc. As one might imagine, this was a bit of a tough sell. However, program officials greatly increased their message's effectiveness when at the end of each session, they asked for a show of hands from all those who committed to serving the new meals. Although the commitment was not binding, the rate of behavioral change increased dramatically when officials asked for the show of hands compared to meetings when they did not.

As this story shows, when you make a commitment to do

something—especially if others see you commit or if you put it in writing—you are much more likely to follow through than if you merely express a desire or you only **think** you will do something. Committing to substitute one or more Virtue for one or more Sin will greatly increase the likelihood that you will measurably improve your relationship to your employees, colleagues, or senior management. If a commitment can induce a housewife to serve pancreatic patties to her children, it will surely promote your putting weight forward on your skis in the workplace!

✓ **Tip 3:** Develop
       a plan.

In his youth, Benjamin Franklin identified thirteen virtues he wanted to practice. Although he committed to all thirteen, he drew up a calendar featuring one each week. As reported in his autobiography, the cycle prompted him to practice them all even as he gave special attention to "the virtue of the week."

Since what gets scheduled is more apt to get done, you can fashion a similar plan creating a cycle with the Eight Virtues. Work on one Sin/Virtue pair at a time. When the Sin-to-Virtue transfer has occurred and your new behaviors have become habit, you can select another Sin/Virtue pair on which to focus. See the Appendix for sample plans.

Your plan may need to identify potential obstacles. For example, if you have been lax in dealing with performance or attendance problems but now commit to D-I-S'ng them, you will be guilty of the fourth form of inconsistency discussed in Chapter Five. Hence, your plan should include the "that was

Journals and Evidence

Although keeping a journal is an excellent tool for making a Sin-to-Virtue transfer, in today's litigious times, a manager should keep in mind that everything in it could end up as evidence if an employee brings legal action. In this context, the journal can be a two-edged sword. If you record reckless, overly judgmental, or emotional comments about employees, the employee may use what you wrote to prove unlawful bias or retaliation. On the other hand, if the journal contains contemporaneous, dated, and accurate notes of facts, such as conversations held with employees regarding Expectations, Responsibility, and Accountability (E-R-A), and if you act consistently with your notes, your journal may furnish important evidence in resolving a "he said/she said" dispute in the company's favor.

then, this is now" message as well as a focus on the Big Picture and why change needs to occur. If you commit to practicing the Sixth Virtue and open information channels, you should assess whether you have built up enough trust with your employees so that the information will not be used as ammunition against you or the company.

In addition to external obstacles, there may be internal ones as well. For example, if certain circumstances invariably "push your buttons," your reaction may undermine your desired change and make you so angry that you can't practice the listening techniques described in Chapter Seven. To achieve the Sin-to-Virtue transfer, you may need to learn an anger-management technique, such as deliberately slowing your breathing. The journal proposed in the next tip will be especially useful as you identify external or internal obstacles and list the steps you will take to overcome them.

✓ Tip 4: Keep a journal.

As Cheryl found, it helps to keep a written record, whether you use it to identify goals, express your commitment, list steps and timetables, or record experiences. Various studies have shown that keeping a journal like this works both the left-brain and right-brain sides of change. With respect to the former, it helps you stay organized, focused, and on track. With respect to the latter, it promotes a sense of confidence and even excitement in the process; it makes you *feel* the change happening. What gets written doesn't always get done, but it greatly increases the odds compared to when you simply think or talk about what you intend to do.

✓ Tip 5: Be a teacher.

One of the best ways to practice the Virtues is to teach them. Teaching others about the beginning-skier instinct versus weight forward on skis, the importance of D-I-S'ng people, or the E-A-R, funnel, or two-for-one listening methods tends to drill these concepts into your own brain. It also reinforces your commitment to do them yourself as a means to bring practice in line with preaching. Keep in mind that your employees may not be your only students. Family members and friends may become willing pupils and further the Sin-to-Virtue transfer process.

✓ **Tip 6:** Get
feedback.

Invariably, there is a danger that you will relapse to former behavior patterns. Also, as Albert Einstein once said, "There is far too great a disproportion between what one thinks one is and what others think one is." To guard against both relapse and a skewed view of your progress, you need feedback. One way to ensure good feedback is to recruit a colleague as your partner. This person can observe changes, encourage and reinforce what is working for you, and offer early warnings if obstacles arise.

Another way is to solicit feedback directly. The Triple Two technique works well here as you ask employees what you should stop, start, or continue doing. Depending on your Sin-to-Virtue plan, other questions could include, "Do you feel you know where you stand with me?" "Do you feel you are able to apply your talents and abilities on a regular basis at work?" "Permission to speak freely: What do you think would most improve our relationship?" Asking such questions periodically will help you remain on the Sin-to-Virtue path. To make sure the questions get asked, you can schedule feedback sessions or set timetables by which you commit to asking the questions of selected employees. Recording your employees' responses in your journal will help you track your progress over time.

Organizational Strategies

Organizationally, a successful move from Sin to Virtue requires a top-down commitment to a weight-forward change in company culture. For such broad-based change to occur, the company's leadership must apply leverage. There needs to be a strong, well-thought-out plan. And there must be substantial follow-up.

How Not to Teach the Sins and Virtues

With backing from the executive committee, the vice president of human resources commenced a program for teaching and applying the Eight Deadly Sins of Mismanagement and Corresponding Eight Virtues. The first session was for the company's officers. The program would then move on down the line to all levels of supervision.

Although the program hit a snag when the CEO left the company, the VP of HR wanted to go forward. Coincidentally, the officers' session was scheduled for the same day that one of the board's CEO candidates would be visiting company offices. The VP saw the timing as an opportunity for the CEO candidate and officers to get a good sense of each other. After first agreeing that the training session should not be postponed, the CEO-candidate decided after he arrived that his time was too precious to "sit in a class." Instead, he had the VP periodically pull senior executives out of the session to meet with him.

Perhaps not surprising, the program proved a failure. The executive team, which had previously supported the program, lost its enthusiasm. Throughout the day, the "revolving door" disrupted presentations and interactive sessions and served as a continual reminder that the program lacked the support of the person who might soon be leading the company. The board subsequently selected this candidate.

He reiterated his view that he did not oppose the program but questioned whether he personally could participate given his other pressing responsibilities as CEO. The program never regained its original momentum. Follow-up sessions were put on indefinite hold, and the program ended in its infancy.

Tools and Techniques

Based on observations of programs that produced positive managerial change and programs that did not, here are tips about steps your organization can take to make the transition from Sin to Virtue and avoid dead-ends or disappointing results.

✔ Tip 1: Make sure the commitment starts at the top.

Organizational change requires leverage. If the desired goal is something more than isolated or sporadic improvements, there must be a commitment at the very top of the organization. The CEO and executive team may approve a program and allocate money and managerial time for it, but these gestures are insufficient if the leaders do not personally take part. They may have other responsibilities that keep them from participating to the fullest. Even so, they must convey the message not only that they want to see the Sin-to-Virtue transition made but that they are committed to learning and applying the concepts themselves. The company's leaders become examples and representations of the change they wish to see in their organization.

✓ **Tip 2:** Identify the Big Picture.

Before launching a new program, a company's leaders should clearly identify the goal. Is it to eliminate certain Sins? Practice certain Virtues? What do they think the desired future looks like? When identifying the core aspects of the Big Picture, it helps to ask questions at all levels of the organization (even of customers and vendors). You can obtain input through a survey as well as interviews conducted by those responsible for the program.

With respect to a Big Picture that assesses the current practices of the organization, questions may include the following:

- For the First Virtue, Weight Forward on Skis: Do employees feel encouraged to own responsibility and take the initiative to solve problems or pursue opportunities?

- For the Second Virtue, D-I-S: Do supervisors promptly let their employees know if there is a problem, and do they recognize or acknowledge employees' positive contributions to the organization?

- For the Third Virtue, Honesty: Do employees and managers sometimes feel compelled to avoid telling the truth?

- For the Fourth Virtue, E-R-A: Do employees feel they know what their boss expects of them and that employees are held accountable for their actions?

- For the Fifth Virtue, Ducks in a Row: Do employees feel they are treated consistently and are expected to treat others consistently with respect to company policy, practice, and precedent?

- For the Sixth Virtue, Open Information Channels: Do employees feel they have the information they need to do

their jobs successfully and management has the information it needs to be successful?

- For the Seventh Virtue, Listening from the Employee's
Frame of Reference: Do employees feel listened to by their
supervisor, co-workers, HR, and senior management?

- For the Eighth Virtue, The Big Picture: Do employees
have a clear sense of the company's mission, vision of a
desired future, goals, and fundamental values?

✓ **Tip 3:** Align current systems
with the program.

To move from Sin to Virtue, a company has to overcome the
inevitable resistance to change. In identifying potential sources
of resistance, take a careful look at existing company policies,
procedures, and practices, all of which you need to evaluate in
light of the goals of the program and desired changes. To
encourage sustained organizational change, you should carefully scrutinize company systems of hiring, orienting, training,
compensating, rewarding, and disciplining employees.

Here are examples of the types of questions to ask:

- Does your performance-evaluation system encourage
supervisors to save up their observations for an annual or
other periodic meeting instead of dealing with issues
immediately?

- Does your compensation plan discourage employees or
departments from sharing information, as did the plan at
the food-processing company described in Chapter One?

- Do you have policies or practices that have grown obso-
lete, that promote inconsistency, or that have lost sight of
the Big Picture?

- Do your employment-law and claim-prevention checklists and programs deal only with technical legal compliance, or do they reflect an understanding of what prevents brainlock?

- Do some of your organizations' managers have firmly held beliefs and practices that conflict with the program's essential tenets?

If you answer yes to any of these questions, the program will not be fully successful unless you overcome these obstacles. Policies and procedures may need to be revised or eliminated. Certain managers may require additional coaching, training, or even a change in job status. The need to overcome obstacles to positive change is another reason commitment from the top is essential.

✓ **Tip 4:** Create the plan.

Based on what the company identifies as the Big Picture, the information it obtains, and core skills or competencies it desires to see instilled, it must formulate a specific plan. Plans will vary from organization to organization and desired outcome to desired outcome. But every company must bear in mind a few basics:

- The company's leaders must communicate the Big Picture. They must provide convincing answers to the question, Why change? They must make clear what is expected, what is important, and why. Finally, they must give the "that was then, this is now" message clearly and repeatedly.

- Managers should avoid overindulging at the "smorgasbord." Every potentially useful management tool or technique has the aroma of a favorite food at the local buffet.

The problem arises when there are just too many appetizers, soups, salads, breads, vegetable sides, main courses, beverages, and, of course, desserts. Twin dangers arise: Managers might overindulge by selecting too many items to consume, or they might become so overwhelmed by the choices that indecision sets in and they don't consume anything. Despite the temptations, you should select only a few core courses from the smorgasbord of possible management tools. You can always choose more after digesting the initial selections.

■ Training should be Just in Time, or JIT. Behavioral training has no shelf life; trainees must either use it or lose it. So teach lessons with the expectation that managers will put them into practice immediately. Otherwise, even the most enthusiastic program participants will find that existing patterns of behavior and rapidly fading memories will erode momentum.

■ A good training acronym is P-I-R-A, meaning Present, Interact, Role-play, and then Apply. It works like this. First the session facilitator presents tools or concepts from the program. Participants then interact, or discuss and analyze them, such as in small groups. Next, participants do role-plays that constitute dress rehearsals for the real thing. Finally, everyone applies the lessons to actual workplace situations. One organization began the move from Sin to Virtue with a one-day session of presentations, interactions, and role-plays. It then set specific assignments and scheduled monthly two-hour follow-up sessions in which "homework" was "graded." For example, with respect to the Eighth Sin/Virtue, the Big Picture, managers had to prepare written statements of their goals. For the Second

Sin/Virtue, D-I-S, they committed to issuing a minimum number of written D-I-Ses for positive behavior as well as to report on corrective D-I-Ses. Participants maintained journals for charting progress, noting examples, and identifying obstacles. As a result, the lessons moved directly into actual workplace experiences.

✔ **Tip 5:** Measure and follow up.

The rule that what gets measured gets done applies to your move from Sin to Virtue. You must start by identifying measuring sticks to distinguish success from failure. Depending on your company size and circumstances, these may include numbers of employee grievances, claims, turnover, absenteeism, workers' compensation experience, productivity, profitability, or numbers of times employees come forward with useful ideas. Measurements may also include evaluating specific management actions—such as administering discipline or evaluating performance—after you've implemented the program. From the CEO on down, managers should be measuring other managers and supervisors in terms of their applying the new tools or concepts; these tools should be part of management's E-R-A and performance evaluation system.

For example, regarding the First Sin/Virtue, Weight Forward on Skis, did management deal with the problem proactively or avoid it for some time? Per the Second Sin/Virtue, were the employees D-I-S'd? Per the Fifth Sin/Virtue, Ducks in a Row, were there inconsistencies in treatment of employees with each other, terms of company policies or past communications? Concerning performance evaluations, did they reflect the "gunnysack" management discussed in Chapter Two, or were they summaries of what the manager had already D-I-S'd?

When describing the success of change initiatives at General Electric, former CEO Jack Welch cited the "relentless drumbeat of follow-up." Identify and agree on benchmarks from competitors, your general industry, or past experience by which you can mark progress. Then, to move lessons from teaching to practice to habit, perform the essential measurement and follow-up. Among the tools that can contribute to the success of your program are 360-degree evaluations, the Triple Two technique, and surveys that focus not on how "good" the training seemed but on what changed. To paraphrase Welch: If you're serious about a Sin-to-Virtue transfer, play those drums!

Chapter Nine Highlights

Transfer of Training

☛ Moving from Sin to Virtue means that employees will transfer the lessons they've been taught to their regular workplace practices and habits.

Individual Strategies

☛ The goal is for each manager to develop habits based on the Virtues.

- Use the instinct to avoid or lean back on skis as a trigger to do the opposite.
- Make a commitment to positive change.
- Develop a plan that includes what you desire to accomplish, steps you will take, resources you will need, and obstacles you will need to overcome.
- Use a journal to record goals, steps, and experiences.
- Be a teacher; teaching the Virtues reinforces your practice of them.
- Get feedback from a training partner or by questioning your employees to ensure that your perception of your transfer mirrors your employees' perceptions.

Organizational Strategies

☛ Organizational change requires leverage, a plan, and follow-up.

☛ The commitment must come from the top leadership in the organization.

☛ Draw a Big Picture. What are the goals of your Sins-to-Virtues program? What is the desired future? What core competencies do you wish to instill?

☛ Align your systems with the desired change. Systems include HR and management policies as well as practices and procedures you may need to revise or eliminate if they run contrary to the goals of the program.

☛ Beware the "smorgasbord" tendency to overindulge by adding too many management skills or competencies to your training program.

☛ Make sure your training comes Just in Time, or JIT. Teach skills when everyone can apply them immediately.

☛ Use a P-I-R-A approach to training: Present, Interact, Role-play, and Apply.

☛ Measure progress and then follow up on it. Assess the program's outcome—in terms of management practices, decisions, and results. Then compare those results to your pre-identified benchmarks.

Conclusion:
Ski the Run!

LESSONS COMPLETE, YOU'RE READY TO face the slope on your own. You snap into your bindings, grip your poles, and adjust your goggles. As you look down the slope, a wave of anxiety washes over you. The self-protective instinct kicks in, urging you to lean back, get your weight up closer to the hill. Yet you remember to treat this instinct as a trigger to do the opposite, so you bend your knees and put your weight forward as you launch yourself out of the gate.

You approach the first flag: signs of discontent among your staff about the new sales quotas. Instead of avoidance ("What a hassle!"), you head straight for it. You listen, gather information, and identify the sources of discontent. Next, you address the issue directly with your employees and mold a consensus on the path forward.

Pleasantly surprised that you're still upright, you approach the second flag: an employee stayed late last night to help a customer. Instead of taking such behavior for granted, you make a point of D-I-S'ng her and following up with a short writ-ten note of appreciation.

With growing confidence in your skiing, you approach the third flag: performance feedback is due for an employee to whom you have told white lies in the past. This time you sit down with him, apologize for your previous lack of candor, and inform him that he is entitled to know exactly where he stands with you. Then you tell him.

Flag four looms before you, and uh-oh!—a dangerous ice patch lies in front of it. A long-term employee has been diag-nosed with cancer and his performance has dropped off dra-matically. You catch yourself leaning back on skis and remind yourself of the instinct to avoid and of doing the opposite. Weight forward again, you develop a game plan with HR and legal counsel to ensure compliance with applicable laws. You express compassion, but you also maintain your manager's E-R-A as you work with the employee to meet and be accountable for performance expectations.

Flag five: disciplinary action needs to be taken against an employee. Instead of simply reacting to the incident, you gather information, review his personnel file and applicable company policies, and inquire whether other employees have been disciplined for similar offenses. With ducks in a row, you initiate disciplinary action entirely consistent with com-pany policy, practice, and precedent.

The finish line is not far away, but first you have to make a scary jump at flag six: the company has unveiled a new compensation plan and you are nervous about your employees' reaction if you reveal its details. Despite your fear, you decide to err on the side of disclosure and share the information. This leads employees to voice some consternation, but they nonetheless view your candor as a sign of respect for them.

You ski over a few bumps near flag seven, temporarily rekindling the instinct to lean back until you catch yourself. One of your employees feels hurt that she was passed over for a promotion. Instead of brushing off her complaint, you invest the time in asking her why she feels that way. You acknowledge her feelings and perspective before responding. Although you can tell she still thinks she should have been promoted, you observe that she shows unmistakable signs of willingness to accept the decision and move on constructively.

Swishing left, swishing right, carving crisp turns in the snow, you head toward the final flag. You confront yourself with the question, Why am I on this course anyway? What is the purpose of my company's existence and of my existence as one of its managers? You look at your department and the employees you manage in relation to the company's Big Picture. You share your vision with your employees and spend time discussing with them the company's Big Picture, theirs, and yours. As a result, your team moves forward together, pursuing a mutually desired future.

You cross the finish line, arms raised. Only then do you realize that the legal system never once got in your way. Congratulations!

Appendix
Tools to Help You Move
from Sin to Virtue

Statement of Commitment

I commit to practicing the following management Virtue(s)

_____

and applying the following technique(s) _____

_____ over the following

period of time, _____.

During this period, I will keep track of the times I practice
the Virtue(s) and avoid the Sin(s) and will observe results.

If practicing these Virtue(s) substantially improves my effectiveness or satisfaction or improves the effectiveness or satisfaction of my employees, I intend to make another
commitment to including additional Virtues and techniques
while I continue to use the ones I have so far been practicing.

_____
Signature

_____
Date

Feedback Checklist

To make the most of a Sin-to-Virtue transfer plan, start with a self-assessment. Next, get feedback from others. If there is a gap between how you perceive yourself and how your employees perceive you, re-examine your self-assessment. Determine which Sin-Virtue pair to work on first and identify the concepts, tools, or techniques in the book that will produce the greatest positive impact.

Sin Self-Assessment

To help decide where to focus first, answer the following questions about each Sin. The stronger the "yes" or the more frequent the behavior, the more that area needs attention.

Sin #1: Managing Like a Beginning Skier

1. Has the fear of a potential legal claim or hostile workplace encounter stopped you from confronting a problem?
2. When you feel a workplace issue will be difficult or painful to address, do you find yourself making excuses for not dealing with it?
3. When things go wrong with an employee, does frustration tend to substitute for action?

Sin #2: Dissin' Your Employees

1. Have you asked someone else to give an employee bad news that you should have communicated yourself?
2. Have you reprimanded an employee with general words or descriptions like "unacceptable," "bad attitude," or "poor," only to have him get defensive and resist your criticism?
3. Have you felt bad because an employee did something positive but you failed either to thank or to praise her?

Sin #3: Rationalizing Away Truth

1. Have you inflated an employee's performance evaluation because you didn't want to discourage him, didn't want a confrontation with him, or worried about a potential lawsuit?

2. Have you been confronted by an employee at an awkward or inopportune time and extricated yourself by falsely reassuring her?

3. Have you had a lousy feeling at the pit of your stomach that you weren't really being truthful with your employees?

Sin #4: Misguided Benevolence

1. Have you felt sorry for an employee and decided to "let things slide" as a result?

2. Have you gotten caught up in an employee's personal problems and found that it impeded your effectiveness as manager?

3. Do you feel that you have not always made your expectations clear to your employees or that you have failed to hold them accountable?

Sin #5: Falling into the Inconsistency Trap

1. Did you change an employee's status—promotion, transfer, demotion, termination—without ever inquiring whether a similar situation had occurred before?

2. Have you made such a status change without checking the employee's personnel file, the employee handbook, and your company's policies and procedures manual?

3. Have you disciplined employees for behavior that you or a previous manager had tolerated but that you felt you

could no longer stand—and failed to give a prior "that was then, this is now" message?

Sin #6: Letting Employees Speculate

1. Have your employees speculated about things they didn't know and drawn conclusions that were worse than reality?
2. Has one of your employees erroneously inferred from someone else's discharge that she will be the next to go?
3. Have you feared sharing information with your employees because of their potential reaction to it?

Sin #7: Listening Through Your "I"

1. Have you cut off an employee's explanation of a problem, only to see an escalation in defensiveness, anger, or hostility?
2. Have you made a negative assumption about an employee's ethics, loyalty, dedication, or competence and later concluded you were wrong?
3. Have you interrupted an employee because you were anxious, uncomfortable, or annoyed with what he was saying?

Sin #8: Front-of-the-Nose Perspective

1. Do you feel caught up in the day-to-day grind, and have you lost a sense of purpose at work?
2. Can you identify your organization's Big Picture (mission, vision, goals, and fundamental values) quickly and with a minimum of mental exertion?
3. Can you identify your own Big Picture quickly and with a minimum of mental exertion?

Overall Self-assessment

Ask yourself the following questions:

- What are my strengths?
- What are my weaknesses?
- What are my biggest challenges?
- What are my biggest opportunities?
- Next, ask yourself about the Triple Two:
  - What two things should I stop doing?
  - What two things should I start doing?
  - What two things should I continue doing?

Your Employees' Assessment

Ask your staff the following questions, giving them permission to speak freely and honestly.

- Do you know what is expected of you on the job?
- Do you feel encouraged to use initiative in solving problems and pursing opportunities?
- Are you getting timely, honest, and useful feedback from me?
- Do you think that I listen to you?
- Do you have the information you need to do your job successfully?

The Triple Two:

- As a manager, what two things should I stop doing?
- As a manager, what two things should I start doing?
- As a manager, what two things should I continue doing?

Looking at Both Assessments

Is there a gap between how you view yourself and how your staff views you? If so, this gap constitutes an excellent starting point for a Sin-to-Virtue Transfer Plan.

Sample Sin-To-Virtue Transfer Plan

The Sin-to-Virtue Transfer Plan is designed to develop a game plan for making the transfer on a specific Sin/Virtue pair. The following is a sample. The **bolded** language prompts you to fill in your own plan.

Selected Sin-to-Virtue Pair:

Sin/Virtue #1—From Managing Like a Beginning Skier to Weight Forward on Skis.

Steps/Techniques:

■ Initiative: confront next employee performance or attendance problem at earliest opportunity.

■ Hold meeting to brainstorm ideas for department improvement and develop implementation plan for at least one idea.

■ Ski Entire Run: although earlier conflict between two employees appears resolved, follow up with each employee to ensure that no embers are smoldering.

Resources:

■ Colleague, spouse, or friend—Explain plan, share progress, get suggestions.

■ Employees—Ask questions from Feedback Checklist focusing on Sin-to-Virtue pair.

■ Reread Chapters One and Nine and use appropriate techniques from other chapters (such as the D-I-S method of communication).

Potential Obstacles:

Internal: Fear/dislike of confrontation and tendency to worry about what could go wrong.

External: Your employees and boss may not understand and may resist change.

Steps to Overcome Obstacles:

- Talk through anxieties with resource coaches. Do role-playing in which, for example, coach pretends to be chronically late defensive employee you have trouble with.
- To reduce anxiety, make list of three worst possible outcomes and what to do to prevent each.
- Use "that was then, this is now" technique with employees, explaining change, reasons for it, and connection to the Big Picture.
- Use Campfire Technique with your boss, explaining how Sin-to-Virtue Transfer Plan ties in to her Big Picture—including her desire for department efficiency and profitability and your plan to stop tolerating poor performance and attendance.

Dates to Measure Progress:

- One week after brainstorming meeting for department improvement: have draft implementation plan to circulate to staff.
- Thirty days after confronting employee about performance or attendance issues: meet with employee to assess and communicate progress.
- Six weeks after first follow-up on employee conflict: follow up again to make sure nothing negative has resurfaced.

- Four months after Feedback Checklist: repeat Triple Two technique with employees to assess whether Sin-to-Virtue transfer has been accomplished.

Weekly Virtue Cycle

This cycle is adapted from Benjamin Franklin's Thirteen Virtues System. To use this system, each week you should focus on moving from the Sin of the Week to its corresponding Virtue. Either begin in the same order as the book or with the Sin/Virtue with highest priority from the feedback checklist. Prepare a Sin-to-Virtue Transfer Plan as shown in this Appendix.

Week 1, Virtue #1: Weight Forward on Skis

Emphasize treating the instinct to avoid as a trigger to do the opposite; take initiative in all things. Ski the entire run by following up.

Week 2, Virtue #2: D-I-S'ng Your Employees

Set numerical goals for D-I-S'ng your employees. Put a battery on your desk or in your pocket to remind you to D-I-S for both positives and negatives. Use the written D-I-S forms in this Appendix.

Week 3, Virtue #3: Making Honesty the Only Policy

Be candid with employees; if you have been less than truthful in the past, apologize and explain they are entitled to the respect of knowing where they stand.

Week 4, Virtue #4: E-R-A, Expectations, Responsibility, and Accountability

Stress E-R-A. Discuss with employees their performance Expectations, their Responsibility for meeting expectations, and their Accountability for results.

Week 5, Virtue #5: Ducks in a Row

Reread the policy manual, handbook, memos, e-mail, performance evaluations, and other documents concerning employees' status. Consult with HR and other managers regarding potential inconsistencies. Take the subjective/objective inconsistency test. Make a special point of being prepared before communicating any message of importance.

Week 6, Virtue #6: Open Information Channels

Ask what information you would need if you were in your employees' shoes, what information you need from them, and who needs to be in the information loop. Then communicate with a view to improving information flow.

Week 7, Virtue #7: Listening Through Your Ears

Select one or more of the six listening techniques and consciously use them at least once per employee that week.

Week 8, Virtue #8: The Big Picture

Identify your Big Picture—mission, vision, values, and goals—in relation to your employees' and the organization's Big Picture; assess alignment with them. Use the Big Picture checklist in this Appendix.

Sample Journal Page

Keep a journal to chart progress, record experiences, and plan next steps. This will greatly increase the likelihood of a successful Sin-to-Virtue transfer. The following sample has **bold** language to prompt your own journal.

Date: June 14, 2005

Summary of Event/Experience:
Sheila was 10 minutes late. Explained importance of receptionist being on time since automatic phone service shuts off at 8:00 and we're in the busy season. Apologized if I had not previously explained importance, but said she needs to make sure she's here by then. She said she understood.

Asked Bill [the boss] about his goals or expectations for my department. He emphasized keeping customers happy while we're stretched thin during busy season. Said I agreed and am applying management techniques from the training program to keep employees focused on what they need to do and nip problems in bud. Said he was glad to hear this and let him know if I need his help.

Held brainstorming session for department improvement. Good suggestions, especially concerning improving information flow. Implement Sam's idea for inter-departmental communication.

Next Steps:

Sheila—monitor attendance. If late again, depending how late and how soon after today, D-I-S her again or implement first step of disciplinary action.

Bill—give him oral report a week from today and tie it to his description of goals and expectations.

Draft memo summarizing brainstorming session, including implementation plan for Sam's interdepartmental idea.

Sample Written D-I-S: Corrective Feedback

This form applies the "List, Meet, Write" technique discussed in Chapter Two. In a quick, easy way, it records communication, protects against claims, and, most important, reinforces your oral message in a powerfully constructive way. Use this form to summarize key points, with emphasis on what needs to happen. The following sample has **bold** language to prompt your own feedback and emphasize important language.

To: Sam Jones
From: Sally Smith
Date: June 14, 2005

This memo follows our discussion this morning. As we discussed, a problem has arisen concerning your not applying the methods adopted in our leadership training program. As you acknowledged, the following methods have not been fully implemented:

1. D-I-S'ng employees on both negatives and positives, as opposed to letting problems build up or taking positive employee actions for granted.
2. Using the Written D-I-S to reinforce important communications (this memo is an example), or for praise.
3. Completing the Feedback Checklist.
4. Preparing a written statement of goals for your department.

Sam, despite the problems, I am encouraged by your recognition of the importance of implementing these steps and your commitment to do so. You said in our meeting that items 1 to 3 would begin immediately and item 4 would be completed within two weeks of our meeting. As I mentioned, I'm here to help, as is Susan in HR.

If you have any questions or if this memo is not an accurate summary of our discussion, please let me know immediately.

Sample Written D-I-S: Praise

This form can be used as a follow-up memo or stand-alone document prepared at the earliest opportunity after observing or learning of an employee's positive action or accomplishment. You want to summarize a *specific* thing the employee did, *when* it was done, the *result* of the action, and the link to your department or organization's Big Picture. Copies should go to the employee's personnel file, to your immediate supervisor, and to anyone else in management who would benefit from receiving it. You may want to personalize your own special forms to make positive written D-I-S'ng quick and convenient. The following sample has **bold** language to prompt your own feedback and emphasize important language.

To: Bill Johnson
From: Sam Jones
Date: June 15, 2005
Cc: Sally Smith, VP
Susan Williams, HR

Bill, I really appreciate your staying late yesterday evening to manually research the Acme Tool account after the computer system went down. Jill from Acme Tool called me this morning thanking us over and over for getting the information to her in time for her budget review despite our computer problems. Because of you, instead of a disgruntled customer, we have one singing our praises!

Your action reflects exactly the Finance Department's goal of not only protecting the company's finances but also maintaining the best customer relations. Thanks, Bill.

Defining the Big Picture

The following questions can help you identify mission, vision, values, and goals for yourself, your organization, and your employees. Then you can assess the alignment among them.

Your Big Picture:
- Aside from earning a living, why do you work?
- Describe a compellingly desirable future for yourself professionally.
- What goals must be accomplished for this vision to be realized?
- What steps need to be taken to achieve these goals?
- What are your fundamental workplace values?

The Organization's Big Picture:
- Aside from economic reasons, why does this organization exist?
- Describe a compellingly desirable future for the organization.
- What goals must be accomplished for this vision to be realized?
- What steps need to be taken to achieve these goals?
- What are the fundamental workplace values here?

Your Employees' Big Picture:
What are the goals, needs, and desires of your employees in finding meaning in work?

Alignment:

- How does your Big Picture fit within the organization's Big Picture?
- How do your employees fit within the organization's and your Big Pictures?
- What steps need to be taken to align yourself, the organization and your employees in terms of the Big Picture?

Creating A Star Profile

Close your eyes and envision a movie that stars your employees. In the movie, you see them engage in, or refrain from engaging in, behavior that relates to the most important aspects of their jobs. View the movie in terms of:

1. Performance;
2. Attendance;
3. Workplace conduct; and
4. The Big Picture.

Now that you've seen this movie, list the critical points that make you smile with satisfaction and feel fortunate to manage such employees. (Use simple, active sentences that take up less than one page.)

Next, use the Star Profile to make better hiring and promotion decisions, to give employees useful feedback, and, if necessary, to replace employees without generating brainlock.

Glossary

Amnesty. An opportunity for employees to have their slates wiped clean and start fresh with new performance expectations when you move from lax to weight-forward management. Consider giving amnesty when all of the following exist: (a) you have repeatedly committed serious sins in your treatment of employees; (b) you are *committed* to skiing the run; and (c) employees receiving amnesty have not committed recent infractions so serious that they legitimately deserve to be disciplined. (Chapter Five)

Big Picture Outline. A means to identify your organization's mission, vision, values, and goals and connect them to your employees' (and your own) job status, performance expectations, growth, and accountability. (Chapter Eight, Appendix)

Brainlock. Employee anger so intense that the person cannot move on, psychologically or physically, without striking back. (Introduction)

Campfire Technique. Asking about the boss's Big Picture and explaining your plans and actions in relation to it. A method by which you can build a more constructive relationship with your boss and gain more autonomy. (Chapter Eight)

Channeling. A technique to avoid an argument with an employee who becomes hostile during a termination interview or other difficult conversation. Instead of being pulled into a debate about why the discharge has occurred, you focus attention on the fact that the employee needs to find a better fit elsewhere. (Chapter Six)

Controlled Disclosure. On sensitive subjects, disclosing the minimum amount of information necessary to avoid speculation and ask employees for their cooperation in keeping the information confidential. (Chapter Six)

D-I-S. A communication technique for giving employees Direct, Immediate, and Specific feedback, both positive and negative. (Chapter Two)

Dissin'. Unintentionally disrespecting employees, adding insult to injury in such a way that you produce brainlock. The word derives from the slang term for speaking to someone disrespectfully. (Chapter Two)

Directive Listening. A technique for making yourself listen even when time is limited or your employee is overly talkative. You control the dialogue and even interrupt as necessary, but you do so with questions designed to direct the discussion to where it needs to be. (Chapter Seven)

Dismiss and Redirect. A technique to use when confronted by employees at an inopportune time. Tell them that what they say is important but can't be discussed at this moment, and then set a specific time when you will discuss it. (Chapter Three)

Ducks in a Row. Covering all the bases before taking a significant employment action. When addressing status-changing decisions involving your employees, ask: Are there any legal potholes I need to be aware of? Have we created brainlock, or are we in danger of doing so? Am I gathering information or actually making a decision? What documents should I read? (Chapter Five)

E-A-R. A listening technique through which you Explore, Acknowledge, (and only then) Respond. (Chapter Seven)

Employment Litigation Post-Mortem. Analyzing a recently concluded employment claim to prevent future claims, improve HR and management policies, and use the pain of litigation to create momentum for positive change. (Chapter Five)

E-R-A. A measure of your supervisory effectiveness at establishing Expectations, Responsibility, and Accountability with your employees. (Chapter Four)

Feedback Checklist. A list of questions designed to identify your worst management habits in areas where positive change would have the greatest impact. (Appendix)

The Funnel. A listening technique through which you ask employees broad, open-ended questions and then narrow their point to its most important element by asking, "Do I understand you correctly that…?" (Chapter Seven)

Initial Employment Period. A policy establishing the first thirty, sixty, ninety, or other number of days of a new hire's employment as the period in which management proactively assesses whether the person-to-job fit is right and employment should continue. (Chapter One)

Instinct to Avoid. A manager's natural, self-protective, and misguided urge to ignore workplace problems or challenges rather than confront them. (Chapter One)

Journal. An ongoing written record you maintain to chart progress, record experiences, and identify next steps, such as when you're working on a Sin-to-Virtue transfer plan. (Chapter Nine, Appendix)

Law of Employee Speculation. A rule of behavior that says if employees don't know about an issue (such as a reason for discharge or the company's plans), they will speculate—and their speculation is always worse than reality. (Chapter Six)

List, Meet, Write. A feedback technique through which you List points for important meetings with employees, Meet with them, and Write a memo to them within one day and on one page confirming the key points of the discussion. (Chapter Two, Appendix)

Misguided Benevolence. Allowing sympathy or compassion to suspend performance expectations and accountability. (Chapter Four)

The Monk. A debate technique for lowering the temperature of a heated discussion. Before disagreeing with an employee's position, summarize it and confirm that you correctly understand what the person said. (Chapter Seven)

P-I-R-A. A training approach with four stages: Present, Interact, Role-play, and Apply to your employees' specific circumstances. (Chapter Nine)

Praise Memo. A letter or note you write to an employee summarizing a specific positive action, when it occurred, the result, and its link to the Big Picture. (Chapter Two, Appendix)

Rationalize. A two-word contraction you can think of as meaning "rational lies." This is an avoidance technique that even managers of integrity use to convince themselves that honesty is not the best policy. (Chapter Three)

Sin-to-Virtue Plan. An organized means to apply the lessons of this book. You select a specific pair of Sins and Virtues and develop a plan for making the transfer. (Chapter Nine, Appendix)

Ski the *Entire* Run. An admonition that once your weight is forward and you're heading toward a problem, challenge, or opportunity, you must keep going. Avoid the tendency to stop short before you see the matter through to a complete and successful conclusion. (Chapter One)

Smorgasbord. The wide array of desirable management skills or competencies you can learn. Just as you should avoid taking too many dishes from a real buffet, you must resist taking on more new skills from a management training program than you can realistically digest. (Chapter Nine)

Star Profile. A list of what a star employee would actually *do* in a particular position regarding performance, attendance, workplace behavior, and the Big Picture. (Chapter Eight, Appendix)

Statement of Commitment. A written expression of your commitment to make the transfer of training. (Chapter Nine, Appendix)

Subjective/Objective Inconsistency Test. A preventive effort to avert problems in hiring, promotion, transfer, pay, or discipline decisions. First ask whether you think there is an inconsistency (the subjective test); then ask whether you can demonstrate that no inconsistency exists (the objective test). (Chapter Five)

That Was Then, This Is Now. A clear message for marking the passage from "then" to "now" when substantial workplace change is about to occur. The point is to let employees know precisely what is going to be different, and why, and how you expect them to change accordingly. (Chapter Five)

Transfer of Training. Taking the management lessons you've been taught out of the classroom and converting them into actual workplace behavior, practice, and habit. (Chapter Nine)

The Triple Two. A feedback technique for yourself. Ask employees: What two things should I (a) stop doing, (b) continue doing, or (c) start doing? (Chapter Seven, Appendix)

Two-for-One. A listening technique through which you deliberately ask two questions of an employee for every one statement you make. (Chapter Seven)

Weekly Virtue Cycle. A self-improvement plan through which you select a different virtue to emphasize in each week of an eight-week cycle. (Chapter Nine, Appendix)

Weight Forward on Skis. A management technique through which you use the instinct to avoid a problem as a trigger to do the opposite of what the urge suggests. (Chapters One and Nine)

Selected Bibliography

BECAUSE THERE ARE SO MANY BOOKS that can help employers make the journey from employment law compliance to better management practice, no list would be complete. However, as a practicing employment law attorney, I have used the following books to help me combine workplace-claim prevention with management and organizational improvement.

Adler, Lou. *Hire with Your Head: A Rational Way to Make a Gut Decision*. New York: John Wiley & Sons, 1998.

Aguayo, Rafael. *Dr. Deming: The American Who Taught the Japanese About Quality*. Secaucus, NJ: Carol Publishing Group, 1991.

Arbinger Institute. *Leadership and Self-Deception: Getting Out of the Box*. San Francisco: Berrett-Koehler, 2000.

Buckingham, Marcus, and Donald O. Clifton. *Now, Discover Your Strengths.* New York: Free Press, 2001.

Buckingham, Marcus, and Curt Coffman. *First, Break All the Rules: What the World's Greatest Managers Do Differently.* New York: Simon and Schuster, 1999.

Carrison, Dan, and Rod Walsh. *Semper Fi: Business Leadership the Marine Corps Way.* New York: Amacom, 1999.

Collins, Jim, and Jerry I. Porras. *Built to Last: Successful Strategies of Visionary Companies.* New York: HarperBusiness, 2002.

Connors, Roger, Tom Smith, and Craig Hickman. *The Oz Principle: Getting Results Through Individual and Organizational Accountability.* New York: Portfolio Publishing, 2004.

Covey, Stephen R. *The Seven Habits of Highly Effective People.* New York: Simon and Schuster, 1990.

Drucker, Peter F. *Management Challenges for the 21st Century.* New York: HarperBusiness, 2001.

Drucker, Peter F. *Managing for the Future: The 1990s and Beyond.* New York: Dutton, 1992.

George, Stephen, and Arnold Weimerskirch. *Total Quality Management: Managing Employees (The Portable MBA Series).* Beverly Hills: Dove Audio, 1994.

Goleman, Daniel. *Working with Emotional Intelligence.* New York: Bantam, 2000.

Johnson, Spencer, and Ken Blanchard. *The One Minute Manager.* New York: William Morrow & Company, 1983.

Johnson, Spencer. *Who Moved My Cheese? An Amazing Way to Deal with Change in Your Work and in Your Life.* New York: Putnam Publishing Group, 1998.

Kelley, Robert E. *How to Be a Star at Work: Nine Breakthrough Strategies You Need to Succeed.* New York: Crown Publishing Group, 1999.

Kotter, John P. *Leading Change.* Boston: Harvard Business School Press, 1996.

Nelson, Bob, and Ken Blanchard. *1001 Ways to Reward Employees.* New York: Workman Publishing Company, 1994.

Peters, Thomas J., and Robert Townsend. *Excellence in the Organization.* New York: Simon and Schuster, 1995.

Peters, Thomas J., and Robert H. Waterman, Jr. *In Search Of Excellence: Lessons from America's Best-Run Companies.* New York: Warner Books, 1988.

Phillips, Donald T. *Lincoln on Leadership.* New York: Warner Books, 1993.

Shula, Don, and Ken Blanchard. *Everyone's a Coach: You Can Inspire Anyone to Be a Winner.* Grand Rapids, MI: Zondervan Publishing House, 1996.

Welch, Jack, and John A. Byrne. *Jack: Straight from the Gut.* New York: Warner Books, 2003.

Index

Jathan Janove, Esq., is a principal of Janove Baar Associates, L.C., a law firm that exclusively represents employers. In his practice, Jathan has developed an emphasis on the intersection of employment-law compliance with best-management  practices. In addition to defending employers from workplace claims, Jathan helps them simultaneously obey the law; avoid legal claims; and create positive, productive relationships with employees.

In addition to the program on which this book is based, his management and workforce programs include "Sexual Harassment & the 55-MPH Speed Limit®," "Top Ten Reasons Employers Get Sued," and "Nuts, Bolts & the Law for the New Manager."

Jathan frequently writes for *HR Magazine*'s "Legal Trends" and "Management Tools" sections and has given numerous presentations to management and HR professionals in the United States and Canada. He is a member of the Anti-Discrimination Advisory Council of the Labor Commission of Utah and of the Society for Human Resource Management. He is a member of the panel of mediators and arbitrators of the National Arbitration Forum. *Chambers & Partners* lists Jathan in its *"America's Leading Business Lawyers,"* describing him as "terrific … in advising clients how to avoid litigation."

For additional information, including some of Jathan's magazine articles, visit his firm's web site at www.janovebaar.com.